D0085819

Voices of Delinquency

for

Schmalleger and Bartollas

Juvenile Delinquency

Edited by

Clemens Bartollas
University of Northern Iowa

PEARSON

Boston   New York   San Francisco
Mexico City   Montreal   Toronto   London   Madrid   Munich   Paris
Hong Kong   Singapore   Tokyo   Cape Town   Sydney

Copyright © 2008 Pearson Education, Inc.

All rights reserved. No part of the material protected by this copyright notice may be reproduced or utilized in any form or by any means, electronic or mechanical, including photocopying, recording, or by any information storage and retrieval system, without written permission from the copyright owner.

To obtain permission(s) to use material from this work, please submit a written request to Allyn and Bacon, Permissions Department, 75 Arlington Street, Boston, MA 02116 or fax your request to 617-848-7320.

ISBN-13: 978-0-205-54446-2
ISBN-10:   0-205-54446-0

Printed in the United States of America

CONTENTS

PREFACE

Voices of Delinquency is made up of twenty-five stories about the delinquent years. This supplement has been revised from former editions and is prepared for Schmalleger and Bartollas's *Juvenile Delinquency* text. Adults wrote most of these stories, as they looked back to their adolescent years. However, institutionalized delinquents wrote three of these stories. To provide a diverse collection of stories, the authors lived in a number of states, had a variety of family and social backgrounds, and committed both minor and very serious delinquent acts.

Some of these individuals tell about childhoods where they did this and that, and they were never caught. Others narrowly eluded police apprehension. Still others were apprehended, tried and convicted, and sent to juvenile facilities. Some adjudicated delinquents decided to turn their lives around, and in later adolescence or early adulthood walked away from crime.

There are other stories here that do not have happy endings. A common occurrence in these stories is that during adolescence or early adulthood, the decision was made to take another's life. These individuals were sentenced to long prison terms; five of these stories are written by individuals serving life sentences for murder. One of these stories is written by an inmate on death row.

Ever since I worked with violent juveniles in an end–of–the–line institution in Ohio during the late 1960s and early 1970s, I have encouraged delinquents and adult criminals to write their stories. With some, it can be a redemptive moment, as they come to grips with a violent act that they have committed on another. With others, they can bring some type of meaning to a life that has had few high moments and a great many sad moments.

These stories ought to be very helpful, especially, in shedding light on the explanations of delinquency and on the environmental influences on delinquency in the text *Juvenile Delinquency*. For example, when you read about the consequences of abuse in the text, several stories bring their own testimony to what an abusive home can mean to a child.

These stories are anonymous for the most part. Several writers, however, did want their names on their stories. It has been my intent to protect the innocent; many of these stories contain information that the writers would not want others to know.

I know the individuals in this book. With nearly all of them, I have a personal relationship. I am pleased that they were willing to contribute their stories to this book.

Acknowledgements

I first would like to express my appreciation to my former editor, Jennifer Jacobson. This book of stories about delinquents was her idea. I am grateful to all of those who wrote their stories for this book.

Editor's Note

The Publisher and Author would like to caution readers about the graphic subject matter and language within many of the stories in *Voices of Delinquency*. Changing subject matter and language would have resulted in a lack of authenticity and would have jeopardized the integrity of each story. This supplement is intended for mature audiences only.

Part I

DELINQUENT ACTS,
BUT NOT THE LABEL

The stories in this part are submitted by individuals who committed delinquent acts but were never caught. What these writers have in common is that they are considered to be socialized individuals. Some are criminology students, some are beginning their careers in other fields, and some of these writers work with adjudicated delinquents.

What Would I Say to Urban Gang Kids?

I was born and raised in Columbus, Ohio. I have spent my entire life until the time of my enrollment in college in an urban setting. In other words, hard core delinquents, gang members, and I come from similar backgrounds.

Growing up for me was an experience that I learned much from. My family was by no stretch of the imagination economically well off. I can remember nights in darkness due to an inability to get the light bill paid on time, times of hunger due to a lack of funds to buy food. There were indeed some rough spots growing up.

In addition to monetary problems, there were family problems for me. I couldn't pick my father out of a crowd because I have no idea what he looks like. My family members have let me down in ways that I do not want to talk about. I was also let down by a number of other people growing up.

However, there were people in my life who gave me direction while teaching me and showing me the path to success. The most important among these people is my mother. My mother instilled in me a sense of dedication to anything positive I set my mind to. She showed me and told me the importance of staying drug–free and the need for obtaining an education.

Parochial Education

When I was five years old and in the first grade, I attended the local elementary school. My mother and new stepfather thought that I should be receiving a better education, so they decided to enroll me in a private school. Undoubtedly, the choice of a parochial school by my parents was meant to serve the role of further indoctrinating me with the principles of Christianity. I was against the school change at first, but as time progressed, I was thankful to them for making the decision. I would not trade the memories I received from attending this school for the world.

This school taught me many valuables lessons, many of which I carry to this day. An example of the change this school brought about in me is in the area of my impulsiveness. When I was young, I used to get urges to do the most inappropriate things. I knew they were wrong, but I had to see how the outcome would be experienced.

The way the school I attended handled incidents of my impulsiveness was in the form of the principal, a Vietnam veteran who stood over six feet tall and wielded a solid wood paddle. He would give me a solid answer as to why I should mend my impulsive ways. The first swat changed my ways for days, perhaps even weeks, but it was the second answer that I received from my stepfather when I went home that began to change me for years.

I also developed a problem with stealing when I was eight years old. I stole a snack from a store while my mother and I were doing the grocery shopping. I don't remember what I stole; what I remember is the gratification I got from knowing I could get any snack I wanted and when I wanted it. For several months, I kept stealing in that fashion until one of the store's employees caught me stealing a pack of bubble gum.

I thought that my stepfather would give me the whooping of my lifetime for this. But it wasn't that way at all. He only put me on a two–week punishment, which turned out to be a hell the likes of which I had not known until then. I could come out of my room only to go to the bathroom and even that was on request. My bedroom was not like the children's bedrooms of today. My parents didn't have to take away a phone, a TV, or even a radio because I didn't have those things anyway. My only source of entertainment was outside my room. I only used my room to sleep in. It was summertime, and I was an eight–year–old confined to a room. Looking out my window, I could see my friends playing and having a good time.

It turned out that one of my greatest memories was when the entire family would sit down together to watch martial arts movies and eat pizza. Even my sister enjoyed watching these movies. In fact, there were a couple of times I think she used some of the moves she had observed to save my butt. On one occasion, a guy in the neighborhood kicked me in the knee and took my football. He was older than me, so I did what I thought was best to do. I got my sister who pretty much bloodied him up and got my football back. I loved her for that. For as long as I could remember, she always protected me from outsiders.

At that private school, I made two important discoveries about myself. The first came from the fact that when I received an A on an assignment, I was rewarded with a king–size candy bar. I cherished candy bars almost more than anything at the time. This motivated me to really take my schoolwork seriously, and for the first time in my time, I began to realize that I had the potential for intellectual achievement in my school work.

My second discovery was that I had the ability to excel in sports, in particular football. When we played football during our lunch break, I would make what seemed to me and the other kids playing the game the most incredible moves before I would score the winning touchdown. In addition, I was strong, really strong, for a kid my age. I was already lifting weights, just because I liked doing it. It was not long before I became involved in little league football.

Public School

I was sent to public school when I was twelve years old. It was a strange environment, noticeably harsher than the one I had just left. Since school uniforms were no longer a requirement, I had the whole issue of what clothing to wear to school. The other kids started to make jokes about my clothing. I got on my mom to buy me the socially accepted clothing for my age group. My mother, however, was very frugal and remains so today. Her resolution to my dilemma was to buy me clothes that were close to the name brand but not quite it.

The kids already knew that I dressed funny but now they knew why. It was that my parents could not afford to dress me like them. In an adult world, this might have drawn sympathy, but in my twelve–year–old world it only drew jokes at my expense. One day I wore new shoes to school. From a distance, they looked like Michael Jordan's tennis shoes. They all started shouting, "Look, he got the new Jordans. Damn, they are sweet." Then, one of them studied my footwear more carefully and exposed me, "Those ain't no Jordans, those is x1200's." To say that I was embarrassed would be a gross understatement. I ran home to tell my mother to take the shoes back and get me some other shoes. I didn't care what kind, just not x1200's.

However, starting somewhere around the age of twelve, I was beginning to feel the company of constant anger and evil thoughts. I would just sit and be mad, and people would always ask me, "What's wrong with you? Who are you mad at?" If I could have trusted anyone at the time with the real answer, I am sure they would have been concerned, because I would have said, "Everything and everyone."

I was mad at my biological father for abandoning me. I was mad at my mother because we were poor and because I was always hungry. I was mad at peers because they played jokes on me and made fun of me. I was even mad at my sister for teasing me. I was mad at my stepfather because he was always disciplining me.

How could I express my hurt? How could I express my hate? How could I make them pay? I didn't know the answer, but I had too much fire in me, fueled by hatred, just to sit around and think on it. So I began working out. I would do push–ups, sit–ups, and shadow boxing in my room until sweat poured from every inch of my body. By the time I was thirteen, I had a bench press and dumbbell set. They were old, but they more than sufficed to let my anger have a go at them. I was also enrolled in classes to teach me how to channel my anger in a constructive manner. In addition, I was enrolled in a karate class to learn to control my emotions while expressing myself in combative form. I took the opportunity now to assault the bodies of my peers. They also struck me back, but I liked the pain.

Finally, what helped me cope with the feelings I had inside of me was that I worked with my stepdad in his grass–cutting business. We would work six days a week during the summers, from about ten in the morning until either the sun went down or we completed our list of customers for the day. One would think I would miss spending the summers with my friends playing games all day, but I looked forward with enthusiasm each morning knowing I was going to spend it with my stepdad while making money at the same time. We had a pretty good thing going for a short time.

Football

High school was a much different world for me. When I heard that a college scholarship could be earned through excelling on the football field, I jumped at the opportunity to play high school football. Although I wasn't the most gifted athlete in my freshman football class, it was clearly evident that I was ready to out work every one in order to better my chances of playing. In addition to working harder during practice time on the field, I also took a liking to the weight room facility.

All this hard work began to yield results on the football field. I was one of the freshman team's defensive dominators in practice and in our games. I even got to play a little in the last two varsity games that year.

I had great plans for my football career my sophomore season. But what was to be a great year for me turned out to be a disaster. I can remember getting yelled at so many times by the head coach for blowing mental assignments. One game I blew about three opportunities for sacks in a row.

After that game I felt so bad I thought about giving up the game of football and doing something else entirely. I told myself I could go one of two ways: either give up football, or come back and fight harder than I have ever fought before to show myself and every one else that I could play the game of football. I chose to fight harder, and my fighting harder began with all my hard work during the summer.

My junior–year season was a transforming point in my football career. I played outside linebacker for our team and looked the part. What was even better was that I had my mind fully in the game. I began to dominate guys across from me and make plays. Now, when I had opportunities for sacks, I didn't let them slip away. I grabbed at the opportunities and slammed ball carriers to the ground. I was becoming a standout. Then, I hurt my shoulder during the last two games of the season, and these two games were not a part of my proudest moments.

My senior-year football season was one that I will always be proud of. I was making plays, my teammates were making plays, and we were winning. In the first round of the state playoffs, we lost, and it was very sad. It meant that my football family would never have the same connections and feelings we once did.

My moment of truth had come. Would I get a scholarship to play football in college? A number of schools came to my high school claiming to be interested in me, but none of them invited me to their campus or made me an offer. My coach went out of his way to help me, and he was instrumental in getting a college interested in me and in giving me a scholarship. I will love him forever!

I had a good football career in college. I red–shirted my freshman year, but I started for the next three years. For my fifth year, I chose to graduate and go on the job market rather than playing another year of football. I was able to find an excellent job as a police officer in an urban department in the Midwest.

Talking to Delinquents and Gang Kids

When I work with delinquents and gang kids as a police officer, I tell them that they should not underestimate the school staff's ability to positively affect their futures. Some of them tell me that there are no positive people in their lives. I always respond that I am willing to bet them that there are.

I tell them that I saw my fair share of criminal activity when I was growing up in Columbus. During that time, the sight of drugs was a constant for me. All of my friends picked up smoking weed and drinking alcohol. I refused to take part in these activities because I knew from the experience of watching others and from talks with my mom and teachers that doing these types of activities would pave the road to failure. In addition to drug activity, there was also a substantial amount of gang activity in Columbus at the time. For whatever reason – economic deprivation, protection, or just something "cool" to do – gang involvement was at its peak. Again, I chose to listen to the people in my life who wished to see me succeed, and I refrained from joining any gangs.

The biggest problem with today's youth is the fact that they do not listen. The youth today think they have life figured out when in reality they are living media and entertainment lies. I communicate to gang youth: You want truth; here it is. The most effective way to tell if you should listen to a person is to observe for yourself where their message has gotten them. A gang will tell you that school is for squares, nerds, or whatever other name they can come up with. Your coach, teacher, or counselor will tell you an education is the most important thing you will ever do with your life.

I ask gang youth: Who should you listen to? Sure, if you join a gang you (might) get a taste of the fast life; however, the end of that decision usually comes quickly. If you end up in prison, consider yourself lucky. The alternative is death. There is no retirement plan. What is worse, there is no family plan for the children you leave behind. Those teachers, counselors, and coaches have gotten their education, and it has gotten them success. Listen and follow the messages of those who wish to make your life a success.

My perspective on gangs is somewhat different than the theories and personal stories I have read and heard before. The central message in many explanations or talks I have heard is that people involved in gangs have no other alternatives than gang life. The neighborhood is tough, they have no money, and it is just too hard to survive without gang life.

I refuse to believe this reasoning. I agree that living in economic disparity and growing up in a rough neighborhood is not easy. However, I contend that there is a way out besides athletic talent or rapping talent. The way is education.

What we must not lose sight of is our history. We are a people who have overcome struggle and adversity. Take, for example, Dr. Martin Luther King Jr. What if he had given in to the pressures of segregation by simply saying "The fight for desegregation is too hard"? What kind of state would we all be in today? What if our ancestors who were subjected to physical slavery had said: "You know the fight for freedom is too difficult; let us give up. There is no way out"?

In our contemporary times, we still have it difficult, but let me assure you, the problems of segregation and slavery make all of our problems seem miniscule. It was against this type of adversity that our ancestors triumphed. Make no mistake: whatever the situation happens to be that you find yourself in today as you sit in a classroom, you can overcome it and be successful. Why? Because the same spirit that existed in the hopeful slave, the same spirit that existed in Dr. Martin Luther King Jr., is the same spirit that exists in you.

If this spirit indeed exists in you, why are you still involved in gangs, crime, and drugs? The reason for this is mental slavery. Mental slavery will say you can't be a success; mental slavery will tell you that you are not smart enough; mental slavery will say there is no hope. Caution – mental slavery will look like your homeboy. Mental slavery will look like your brother, your mother, your father, or your friends. But the message of mental slavery is easily detected because it bears no positive outcome. In the words of Bob Marley, "Emancipate yourself from mental slavery; none but ourselves can free our minds." Think on this. For years, our people have crawled through mud, shit, and piss and came out clean on the other side. Why stop now?

In order to fulfill our purpose of success, we must be educated. Do not believe the lie that you do not have the ability to learn. The structure of the human brain ensures you can. Do not say my school is no good; I can't learn there. Listen not to the lie that college costs too much. Many people have dedicated their lives to make sure ample numbers of scholarships, loans, and grants are available.

Also, it might be a good idea to find legitimate employment. Yes, you can get a job; do not listen to the lie that you can't. Most importantly, do not listen to mental slavery when it says to you, "Going to college is not my way. It's not keeping it real." I assure you, it is your way because it is our way, and from Eli Whitney to Cornel West, it's our way. So keep it real!

I close by telling that I chose not to become involved in criminal activities because I took to heart the things I have shared with you. I urge you to do as I have done and listen to a person who is trying to help. I remind these gang youths that it would be a great thing if they felt good about what they were doing with their lives, and that their children and grandchildren would be proud of their successes and achievements.

CRITICAL THINKING QUESTIONS

1. What were the main turning points in the story of this author's life?
2. How is his life similar to and different from urban youths who become involved in drugs, gangs, and delinquent activities?
3. What does this individual mean by "mental slavery"? What do you think of this concept?
4. How do you think students who are gang members would respond to what the author has to say?
5. Does the fact that this individual is physically imposing, mentally sharp, and verbally articulate make his speech more plausible?

2

A Naïve Offender

If asked if I engaged in delinquent behavior as an adolescent, my automatic response would be no. Yet upon pondering the question deeper, I would have to say yes. I would have been in deep trouble if I had been caught. I've never considered myself a troublemaker, quite the contrary. Actually, I've always thought of myself as a dedicated student and a well–behaved individual who endured many tribulations throughout my adolescence, but who has usually managed to follow the path of what is right.

I grew up in a small rural town in Iowa. When I was eight years old, my mother left my father, leaving my younger brother, Aaron, and I to remain with our father. A few years later she moved away with a boyfriend to Florida where I only saw her for a few weeks every summer. My father struggled as a single father trying to raise us and make enough money to support us. We were fortunate to get some assistance from food stamps, a food drive, and T19 insurance.

He went to community college to prepare himself with skills for a better job. He was not around much since he was also working two odd jobs for some extra money. I know that he loved us very much, but he was not very good at showing his feelings for us or giving us a lot of parental guidance. It was especially hard for me to not have a female figure in my life.

When I was about twelve, my father met Denise. She soon moved into our home with her three–year–old daughter from her first marriage. She seemed very nice at first, but then she began to cause a wall to form between my father and me that has never gone away. I am not sure why or how it started, but she soon began to make up stories of things that I supposedly did or caused me to always get blamed for everything, whether I was at fault or not. Soon, there wasn't a day that went by without my father yelling at me for something. He became very demanding and was always making me explain my actions to him. I began to get very defensive in my attempts to always explain or try to show my father that I wasn't at fault or didn't mean for it to happen. Yet, even that got me into trouble. I was labeled as mouthy and often was slapped for my behavior.

I remember one such instance where Denise had baked cookies and my father told me not to eat any until after dinner. I don't know if I was just absent–minded or what, but a while later I ate a cookie. I swear I did not go intentionally against their wishes, but there was no way to try to explain that to my father.

Denise went downstairs to my father and told him, and soon I heard the foreboding thud of his footsteps pounding up the stairs. He asked me what my problem was and I asked him what he was talking about. He demanded to know why I went against his orders and ate a cookie, but I couldn't make him understand that I forgot or was just absent–minded and hadn't really thought about it when I grabbed a cookie. He grew angry with me and advanced towards me to slap me. I knew it was coming by the look on his face and grabbed a pillow off the sofa to block his hands. In our struggles, he fell on top of me. Upon hearing the commotion, my brother rushed out and pinned my father to the floor telling him to get off me. Yet, the thing I will never forget is the cocky grin on Denise's face as my father was yelling at me. It was almost like she was enjoying it.

My jaw would hardly open very far, due to the bruises and swelling from my father slapping me. I talked to a nurse who called my dad, but that is all the school ever did. They were aware of the difficulties I was having at home, but they never tried to help eliminate the problem.

Nothing I did was ever good enough for him and I began to dread coming home from school. I didn't have many friends when I was younger. I was very shy and quiet. I also became very self–conscious, mostly due to the verbal abuse I received from my father. It made me question a lot of things about myself. Other kids began to poke and tease me because they knew I was an easy target to pick on. I didn't feel like I belonged anywhere. I had to wear worn–out clothing from a consignment shop that my grandmother would buy me, while other classmates were wearing the latest fashions. I was very jealous of the few friends I had for having a close family that loved them and cared for them.

The fighting only grew worse and more constant, and two days after my fourteenth birthday, I ran away. I didn't know where I was going, but the only thing that was important to me was getting away. A few hours later, my Aunt found me walking late at night toward a nearby town. I stayed with my grandmother until I went to spend the summer with my mother in Florida. Upon returning to Iowa, I went and lived with my father's sister, who lived in a large town about five hours away.

It was quite an experience for me just starting high school in a large town where I didn't know anyone. My classmates were very friendly, boys began to notice me, and I became "popular," which is something I wasn't used to. I really liked living here, but missed my younger brother, Aaron, a lot. Things seemed to be going very well here, and I was happy for the first time in a long time.

Then one Friday, unexpectedly, things did a complete turnaround. My father and Denise came to my school to pick me up for what I assumed was to be a weekend with them. I began to get homework out of my locker and then my father took me into the office to check me out. The principal was there and made a remark about enjoying me as a student, but at least I would be warm. I was confused by what he said and asked my father what he meant. He told me to make sure I emptied my locker because I wouldn't be returning. They were driving me to Florida tonight to have me live with my mom.

I began crying and felt so hopeless at having no power to convince them to let me stay. It saddened me deeply because I was so happy and didn't want to leave, and they didn't want to give me the chance to say goodbye to my friends for fear that I would run away again. I was so scared of living in Florida where I didn't know anyone and would be so far away from everyone I knew.

Upon returning to my aunt's home, I cried and begged my dad to let me stay. He told me I only had two options; I either live with my mother in Florida or I go to a mental hospital. That really made me hysterical. I screamed at him that I am not crazy and how could he even think that I needed to go to a place like that. Apparently, it had been Denise's idea. Not very surprising to me. I called my mom and she told me that I should just go with them to her place. I became so numb and oddly calm, knowing I had no real choice. I was able to convince them to let me return to the school to at least say goodbye to my friends before I left.

Living at my mom's was actually nice. I was able to build a stronger bond with my mother than we had before and was able to make a lot of new friends there also. Yet, the only thing I could not stand was being away from my brother, Aaron, who I am very close to. So when I went back to Iowa to visit for the following summer, I knew I couldn't leave my brother again, despite the hardships I knew I would face at my dad's.

Of course, things soon went back to where they were before with me and my father and stepmom. (My father married Denise while I was in Florida, but I had refused to come back for their wedding because I felt that he was making a mistake. I think he felt compelled to marry her due to my little brother, Allen, who they'd had together.) Denise was also going back to school and upon her internship, had convinced my father to let her live an hour away where she was doing her internship. Things were falling apart for them and she soon left my dad for another man she was having an affair with. In fact, upon the day of their divorce, she was in labor with this man's child.

My father turned to alcohol as a solution to his troubles. He was coming home drunk every night and passing out on the sofa. His temper was worse and I tried to avoid him as much as possible. It was tearing me apart to watch him like this. We were fighting more severely, mostly due to my concern for him.

When I was growing up, I tried to advance myself through school by getting high grades and being involved in school activities to help me achieve success in school as a way out of my life. I also read a lot of romance novels. They were an escape from my troubles. I was able to lose myself in the book and become part of the plot. I would often dream of meeting someone wonderful who could take me away from my life and make me happy. Two days after my sixteenth birthday, I thought I had met this man.

His name was James and he was the sweetest, most caring man I had ever met. He was my "Prince Charming." It was a story of a small town girl and a big city boy. He seemed so worldly to me and he really seemed to care for me. He would buy me roses for no reason at all, constantly opened doors for me, wrote me poems, always complimented me and told me how beautiful I was, etc. He made me feel very special.

When I was seventeen, I was in a severe car accident. I was in a coma for a week and hospitalized for two months. I suffered a head injury and had to undergo a lot of therapy. I would never be the same person I was before. Things that were easy for me before were now very difficult. I was extremely fortunate to still be alive.

A week after my release from the hospital, James proposed to me. I was so scared; I was only seventeen, a senior in high school, still trying to adjust to how my accident had changed me. I didn't want to make the same mistake my parents did. My head was screaming no, but my heart was telling me how he was there every day in the hospital for me. I didn't know what to do, so I said yes. Two days later, I broke it off. I old him that I still wanted to be together, but I wasn't ready to be that serious. He took it to mean that I didn't want to be with him anymore, and I didn't see him for about two months.

We did get back together later and things seemed really good between us. A lot of people didn't like him because he was different than most of the people in my school. There were rumors that he was in a gang, did drugs, etc. James always denied this, and being naïve and in love, I trusted him. I knew that he had sold and used drugs in the past, but he told me I changed him and he gave that up. He did however have friends in the Gangster Disciples, but he swore he was never a member. All I ever saw was the good in James and never really felt it was bad that he had friends in a gang. Maybe I was more tolerant due to all I had seen and experienced from living in Florida? Maybe I was just scared of being alone?

His life was always intriguing to me. Sometimes we would go to the city, which was an hour away, and cruise the strip. I met a lot of his friends and the life there was much different than mine. I remember one time when my brother, Aaron, came with us and we pulled over to talk to some people that James knew that were Gangster Disciples. One particular person was Cleo, who was very intimidating and had a sense of power about him. We were standing beside the river and Cleo told James he was going to throw me into the river and wanted to know what James was going to do about it? James told him, "nothing" and I remember thinking, "What does he mean – nothing?" I did not want to be thrown into the river and was a little intimidated by the situation so I remained quiet, which surprises me now considering how defensive I can be.

When James said he wouldn't stop him, Cleo started laughing and the subject was then dropped. After we had left, I demanded to know what all that was about. James explained to me that it was about respect. Cleo was testing James's respect for him and the gang. If he had tried to stop him, Cleo would have thrown me in, and probably James in, too. It was a lesson I don't think I will ever forget.

On my eighteenth birthday, following my high school graduation, my father told me he wanted me out of the house. James and I were able to find a mobile home to buy and we lived there for about a year. After two months, James proposed again and I gladly accepted. I was in college and wanted to wait a while, but we still began to plan for the wedding. It was about seven months after his proposal that I discovered the hidden truth behind our relationship.

James had been lying to me for a very long time and was not only using drugs, but also selling them to my brother's friends. I can't even explain how I felt inside. I was so hurt and betrayed. How could I have not known? How could he have lied to me about it? When I confronted him with my knowledge of his actions, he said he was sorry and would change. I loved him so much; I wanted desperately to believe him.

Not too long after that, James told me that he needed to smoke marijuana once in a while, due to the stress from his job, but when we moved in a month and a half, he would quit. I gave in and said it would be okay, despite the fact that I hated it. When it came time for us to move to the city for us both to go to college there, he continued using marijuana and, I strongly suspected, other drugs. He would lie to me and sometimes not even come home when I had no idea where he was. When he was gone for a whole week without returning, I became more concerned than usual. His behavior was tearing me apart and I was extremely unhappy. I called his best friend and discovered that was where James was staying, but he wouldn't talk to me. I tried to go over there to talk to him, but he left in his car. While I went to the gas station, he returned and refused to let me in to talk to him. I didn't know what was going on and had nowhere to turn.

About a week later, I stopped where he worked and he grew angry with me for stopping to talk to him. He yelled at me and said he didn't love me anymore and we're over. I begged him not to and told him I loved him, but he wouldn't listen. I was crushed. All my dreams were now gone and I had no idea where to go now.

I was able to find different places to stay in the city, but finally moved back home while I was going to college. I still talked to James every once in a while, but he was usually distant toward me. On rare occasions he would be sweet to me, which only managed to confuse me more. All I could think of was our good times and how badly I wanted him back. I didn't want to admit to myself that it was better for us to be apart and that he was not the same person I fell in love with. He went against every value I had. He "socialized" me into thinking it was okay to change these beliefs into ones that he felt were more acceptable for the lifestyle he liked to lead.

By my wanting James back so badly and my willingness to do about anything to show him how much I cared for him, I was easily misled into doing things that went against what I stood for. James would sometimes go to Chicago with Omar and Mike to buy drugs. It made me worried about them and I didn't like the idea of them taking a bus into such a rough neighborhood. Therefore, when they were planning another trip, they talked me into driving them. I agreed out of my concern for James. I felt that, if I did it, maybe he would see that I could be more down with what he was doing.

It has to be one of the dumbest and scariest things I have ever done. It was about 3:00 a.m. when we got there and it looked like such a rough neighborhood. Everything looked worn down and we couldn't get a hotel since three of us were white, but Omar had a niece over on Halstead Street, who he said would let us stay with her. James talked me into giving him $100 to buy some stuff and I only agreed since I knew he was being paid next week. He knew he could talk me into doing just about anything for him. Mike and I stayed with Omar's niece while James and Omar took my car to get the goods. When it was a couple of hours after they were supposed to be back, we were all very worried that they had been killed or arrested. Finally, they came back, breathless and with blood on their clothing.

James told us that while they were waiting outside a house, a car drove by slowly. He said it returned and a guy got out running toward them and shooting at them. Omar and James took off running in different directions. James said he was able to get back to my car and drove around looking for Omar. Omar had cut a huge chunk out of his leg when he jumped over a barbed wire fence while he was running. I was just so thankful that they were both alive and okay, that I wasn't that upset that they were late.

They still hadn't gotten any drugs, so before we left to go back to Iowa, we pulled over to where Omar got out to talk to some people and he came back asking me for $50 more. I didn't like the idea that I had already given $100, so I refused. Omar explained that if we didn't pay them more they would kill us or seriously injure us. I didn't know what to do and since I had no doubt they would do just as Omar said, I gave him $50 more, with the stipulation that they had to pay me back my $150. Omar bought some cocaine and we pulled over to his sister's house where he went and with the help of Vaseline, hid the drugs inside him, in case we were to be pulled over. It amazes me what people will do for drugs.

We made it back to Iowa okay and were extremely lucky not to be arrested. At the time, I never thought of the consequences, but now I know I could have gone to prison for my actions since I was the one who drove and gave them the money for the drugs. I am so fortunate to still be here!

About two months later, it was still bothering me to be without James. I began to go out every weekend and was drinking a lot, as if that would make me feel better. I was so depressed I even asked James to let me try to get high since I heard it would make you happy. I was so desperate to forget my pain and to just be happy again. I tried it, but it didn't affect me. I tried it five different times, before I got high, and then I never tried it again. I was deeply ashamed with myself for trying it. I even bought a dime bag from James for a friend who also wanted some because she was depressed, but didn't want anyone to know it was for her.

James dropped out of college and moved with a friend back to my hometown. I knew I needed to get away from him or I would never get over him, so I moved back to the city with a cousin to finish my last year at the community college. The distance did me a lot of good.

I didn't really date for about two years after James and I broke up. Mostly it was because I was scared of being rejected. I felt like everyone important in my life had rejected me, from my mother leaving us, to my father never being happy with anything I did, to James abandoning me. Also, I'm scared of being alone and can be too trusting of people. I didn't want to latch on to anyone just so I wouldn't have to be alone again.

I needed to make a new life and needed new friends. I wanted to be accepted and to fit in. I always somehow managed to get in with the wrong crowd though. I became involved in the student senate and other student activities on campus, and through my activities, met a few friends who seemed to be very popular with everyone on campus. Ben was very outgoing and quite friendly. He was also very persuasive. He had the master key to all of the departments on campus and had constantly asked me to come with them to break into the warehouse of the bookstore to steal clothing and books to sell back to the bookstore for profit. I always refused, but one evening I gave in. It was quite a rush sneaking in the back door late at night and looking around for campus clothing and books to take. We all rushed back to the car with our adrenaline flowing like we had just accomplished some major feat, but in reality I felt awful. The whole time I kept waiting for security to catch us and then I would be expelled from school and who knows whatever consequences I would face. This would be very bad, especially since I was going after a law–related degree.

Yet, I must not have learned my lesson very well. I was a work–study in the media department on campus and I helped Ben to steal a TV from our warehouse in the basement. I don't know why I did it, especially since I didn't even get anything out of it. Plus, I paid Ben $50 to steal me a VCR. I still felt awful after doing this and was very confused about where my life was headed.

All of my actions made me feel awful about myself and I knew I couldn't go on like this. I concentrated harder in my studies, achieved straight A's, and managed to graduate at the top of my class with a two–year degree. I was also given an award for being an outstanding student.

I have transferred to a university, where I am now majoring in criminology. Upon completion of my bachelor's, I plan to get my master's degree. I really want to do probation so I may help others onto the right path. I have learned a lot through my experiences and have managed to make my relationship with my father a little stronger. My family is important to me and I would do anything for them.

(All of the names have been altered due to the circumstances and my need to remain anonymous.)

CRITICAL THINKING QUESTIONS

1. What is a naïve offender?
2. If she were caught at the wrong time (for example, when drugs were in the car), what do you think would have happened to her?
3. What mistakes did she make along the way?

The Athlete

I was born in 1978 in Iowa. My life started out pretty interesting right at the hospital. There was another couple there that had a baby boy the same day I was born. The father happened to overhear that my dad was expecting a boy because that is what they said I was for the last three months of my ultrasound. The father looked over to my dad and offered to trade his son for me because he only wanted girls, no boys at all. My dad said, "No way." The other man said he was very disappointed in his wife because she did not have a girl. So the day I got to leave the hospital with my correct parents, that woman sat and waited for her husband, who never came for her.

After a couple of years my dad got transferred to work at a different plant. It was about this time that I became very infatuated with horses, so my parents bought me a "Wonder Horse," which is a type of rocking horse. I rode my horse all the time and rarely shared it with anyone. I would wipe him down with wet washcloths and even brush his teeth with my toothbrush and toothpaste.

When I started sixth grade I still had the feeling of not quite fitting in. Throughout the year I gained some weight, but most of it came when I broke my ankle. I had to wear a cast for six weeks because I had chipped a bone spur off the side of my ankle that was partially connected to my muscle. After that, I picked friends that had weight problems similar to mine.

Seventh grade started off okay, but not great. I lost a little weight over the summer, but it started to come back once school started. I still hung out with my friends who were supportive of the way I was, but I still felt very insecure. My parents noticed the way I was acting. My dad decided I needed something to make me feel positive about myself. My dad came to me one day and said we were going to buy our own show horse. We didn't have a large budget like the doctors' and lawyers' daughters, but that was half the challenge.

Buying my horse really helped my self–esteem. I lost some weight and made some really nice friends during second semester. I did a lot more things that summer with more people. I even decided to go out for sports. My dad coached basketball and thought it would be fun for me to try. So he helped me practice. Although I hadn't played that often before, I started for eighth-grade basketball. I became friends with a teammate and we became inseparable. I lost quite a bit of weight and got taller that winter and I was excited, because that spring I was going to be able to show my horse.

Spring came quickly, and before I knew it, we were at the Spring Show in Des Moines. I was very nervous about showing. I could hardly breathe as we entered the arena for my first class. It went so smoothly that I didn't care if I even won a ribbon, but I did. I won first place. I couldn't believe my ears. I won second class and was Reserve Champion in the Championship class. I had so many people congratulating me. I was so amazed. For the first time in my life I realized what I was capable of and that I could be number one.

My freshman year of track was amazing. Our relays qualified for the Drake Relays. We won second place in the 4 by 100. We also did very well at State that year and won second place in the 4 by 100 and third place for the Sprint Medley. I continued to do well in showing my horse; I was consistently winning first place.

That summer after school let out, I took my track coach's advice and started lifting weights. I also started doing plyometrics with some of the football players. I wanted to be twice as good at track in my sophomore year. I continued spending time with my friends, and riding, and showing my horse throughout the summer. I decided to try cross-country when school started, to be in shape for basketball that winter and track in the spring. The cross-country program has a running club called Hill Toppers that meets at the end of each summer and gets everyone used to running distance again. It was something I was not looking forward to that much, because there is a big difference between two miles and 100 meters. I ran cross-country that year. I wasn't that good at it, but I had fun. It gave me a chance to meet the distance runners. I went into the winter basketball season that year in really good shape. We had to run mountains and I would always be the first one done. Our team was really good that year and I was one of the starters for the sophomore team.

That was the winter I started to get in a little bit of trouble. I knew some kids that were known for being partiers, even though they attended a Catholic school. I started hanging out with some of the kids I had gone to elementary school with. They would come watch me play basketball and we would go out afterwards. One night, after one of my games, we stopped at a grocery store. The guys I was with told us to get bottles of Snapple lemonade. When we got back into the car one of them showed us a bottle of vodka that they had stolen. I never drank before in my life. They showed us how to pour out half of the lemonade and mix the vodka in with the juice. By the time we had gotten back to Cedar Falls, I was feeling a little bit of a buzz. We decided to stop at the popular hang–out for the high school students. When I got out of the car to go to the bathroom, I almost fell on my face because I was quite a bit more buzzed than I thought. I was sort of embarrassed because I remember people trying to talk to me and saying that they couldn't believe that I was drunk. After I went to the bathroom, we left. I did this a couple of more times until one night I drank too much and got really sick to my stomach. After that happened, I decided drinking was not my cup of tea and I could do without it.

I had a bunch of fun my sophomore year of school. I hung out with all the popular kids that played sports. I had a couple of nice boyfriends at the beginning, but I was still pretty shy. Then a senior asked me out, and we started dating. I was feeling pretty good about myself at this time. By the end of the school year, I had a summer of fun planned. My boyfriend and I decided to stop seeing each other because he was going away to college and we wouldn't be able to see each other that much. We still stayed friends though. Then I got a crush on this guy in my class named Tom. I started hanging out with his group of friends more and more, so I could hang out with him. The bad part about hanging out with them is that they liked to smoke pot and drink all the time. I still didn't drink, but I tried smoking pot. I liked it much better than drinking because it didn't make me sick. The more that I hung out with these kids, the more I kept smoking. My parents were pretty lenient with my summer curfew; as long as I called, I could stay out until very late. Soon I was hardly hanging around with my old friends any more. I didn't notice because I had started dating Tom and was too involved with the relationship. My dad hated him and told me he preferred that I didn't date him. He said that he could tell Tom was nothing but trouble. At the time, I didn't think my dad knew what he was talking about. I kept dating Tom. By the middle of the summer one of Tom's older friends had a new party favor for us to try. So the whole group of us started using crank. The whole group of us would snort it and stay up all night for several days. I stopped working out that summer and decided not to go out for cross–country that fall. The summer of partying had left me in not so good shape and had made me lazy. I decided swimming sounded easier.

Swimming wasn't as easy as I had anticipated it would be. The coach was just as intense as our cross–country coach so workouts were extremely tough, and not to mention very early in the morning. We would practice twice a day once the school year began. I could only take it for two weeks, and then I quit. I thought that I would still be able to run track as well as I had before. I continued to party and do drugs. By basketball season I was really out of shape. I hadn't practiced very hard for that either. I did real poorly at practice and found it very hard to be there. It was weird because I wasn't really good friends with anybody anymore.

My parents began to notice my odd behavior. I was snorting a large amount of crank now. One night when I came home they went through my purse and found a quarter gram of crank. I lied and told them it belonged to this kid I knew. They said I couldn't hang out with him anymore. My behavior must not have stopped, because a week later they searched my purse again and found another quarter gram. They reported it to my school counselor and had me evaluated. I promised I would stay out of trouble from now on after they decided I wasn't severe enough for inpatient treatment. I did get kicked out of basketball, and they weren't sure if I would be allowed to participate in track. I felt really helpless at this point in time, like I was lost. The administration decided that since my parents had reported my incident, I would be able to run track. I was very relieved.

That track season didn't start as well as those in the past. My coach was given another job at a different high school because it was where he taught. I didn't hit it off too well with my new coach. He added fuel to the fire when he accused me of smoking cigarettes, when I, in fact, had severe pneumonia. I ended up missing over a week and a half of school because of it, and it made me very weak. Right after I had recovered from that, I began to get real sick in the morning before school. I scheduled an appointment with my doctor and I learned that I was pregnant. This came as a real hard blow. I decided not to tell my parents and take care of the problem myself. I told Tom and he was a jerk about it. We had already been having a rocky time in our relationship. I suspected him of cheating on me and he wouldn't tell me the truth. I decided to have an abortion. Meanwhile, track was becoming harder and harder to run without getting fatigued. I was trying to find out where to go to have the abortion and then figure out how to get the money. It took me a while to find out where to go. I had to have a girlfriend of one of Tom's friends help me find out where to go. Tom just kept procrastinating. It was becoming very frustrating for me. My performance in track fell and I started to gain weight. I was almost three months pregnant when I got my appointment scheduled. My dad even asked me once if I were pregnant and I lied to him and said no. Tom borrowed his mom's car that day and we drove to Iowa City for the appointment. I was very nervous, and all Tom did was smoke pot on the way down with his buddy who came with us. When we got there I checked in at the front desk. As soon as I was checked in, Tom said he didn't want to wait there and he would have more fun walking around. His friend looked at me as they were leaving and said he was sorry they were leaving and hoped I would be okay. I had to wait almost four hours for my abortion. Tom didn't even check with me for almost three hours. I felt very angry and scared. I knew Tom genuinely didn't care about anyone but himself at that point in time. When I went back they gave me an IV for the pain. After it was done I went to the recovery room. They gave me juice and cookies to snack on. I threw them right back up. The IV didn't agree with my system very well. When the nurse came back with some water for me I could hear him out in the lobby asking a nurse to get me because he was ready to go. I tried to get up to get my clothes on to leave. The one nurse asked what I was doing, and after I told her, she said she didn't think I was ready to yet. She told me what she thought but said she couldn't force me to stay. I went into the bathroom to change. I puked again and was extremely dizzy. It was hard to get dressed and took me awhile. The nurses finally had to help me finish and walk me to the lobby. They told Tom he would have to help me; he only helped me out of the building and then his friend had to help me. He said he was pissed it took so long and he was hungry. We stopped at McDonald's on the way home. I tried to eat but got really sick. I had to sit on the toilet for over five minutes because I was bleeding so badly and the dizziness still hadn't worn off. It was all I could do to get back to the table. After we left the restaurant I laid down in the backseat to rest. I had taken my drink with me and accidentally spilled some of it when we made a sudden stop. Tom looked back at me and yelled at me for spilling my drink. I had just about had enough at that point. I still kept dating him though. I felt guilty for what I had chosen to do, but I was also very relieved.

My senior year I had toned down quite a bit, which is surprising because that is the year my parents got a divorce. I went to live with my mom. I decided to put my efforts back into sports, although I did continue to smoke pot occasionally. Basketball went all right, but I was not as good as I had been in the past. I felt like an outsider most of the time because I wasn't close to anybody on the team. Track was just as disappointing for me. My speed was not there like it had been in the past, and instead of being the track star I was just mediocre. That was the hardest blow to take.

Then one day I was talking to my brother's friends and they were talking about their boxing tournament they had gone to. I became interested in trying something new. Tom was very opposed to the idea and that fueled me even more to go. I had become dependent on him since I had limited myself to his group of friends. I knew I was unhappy, but was not strong enough at that time to leave. I let him walk all over me like a rag doll. I went to boxing and met with the coaches. I was intimidated at first because I was the only girl. Everybody was pretty nice, so I became more comfortable after awhile.

With track it was hard to go consistently to boxing so I didn't compete in any tournaments. We were a week away from our state–qualifying meet. There was a girl whom I had been having problems with for the last couple of years in school. I guess she was talking crap about me and it made me mad. I dwelled on it for a while and decided to do something about it. I went into the class we had together in the morning and walked up to her. I called her a bitch and then I punched her square in the nose. I literally smashed her nose. I had to go to the emergency room as well because I hit her so hard that I broke the skin open on my hand and had to get stitches. I got in serious trouble for doing that and was suspended from school for a whole week. That meant that I would miss the state–qualifying meet and not be able to run at the state track meet. I felt horrible, not for what I had done, but that I blew my second chance. I eventually decided to deal with that fact and move on.

That summer I partied moderately, which consisted of driving Tom around because he was drunk and smoking pot. I enrolled at the University of Northern Iowa for the fall semester. Tom wasn't exactly too excited about that, but I didn't care because it was coming from someone with only a tenth grade education. I basically blew him off because I knew he wanted to pull me down to his level. I saw it as a way to get away from him.

I started boxing three or four nights a week and lost about ten pounds from it. I was getting ready for my first fight that December. I remember seeing Tom out at one of the bars around this time. I couldn't believe I stayed with him so long, because he was so rude. That gave me even more motivation to work hard at boxing because it was something he didn't want me to do.

I had my first fight in December. I was very nervous about fighting because it was something that I had never done before and I didn't know how I would do. The moment I stepped into the ring it was like a whole different world. All I saw was the girl that I was fighting. She got some good punches off on me but I was surprised at how well I fought skill- and strength-wise. I ended up winning my fight. I was so pumped after that. It was such an empowering moment for me.

It was around late January when I started getting into snorting coke and crank again. Some of the people I was hanging around with were starting to get real heavy into it. For a month I hardly slept or ate anything. I was doing so much that I lost over twelve pounds in a matter of two weeks. Some of my friends that I worked with knew what I was doing and told me I needed to get my act together. I did about the end of February in just enough time to get ready for Golden Gloves. From starving myself I gained back my weight and a little extra so I moved up a weight class. I was nervous because I knew I was not in very good shape. I ended up fighting a girl with more experience than me. I went into the ring to fight her. She was giving me dirty looks and trying to intimidate me. That pissed me off real bad. I had to beat her if it killed me. She used her size to her advantage against me which made it real tough to fight her, but I out-skilled her and won the fight. It was so awesome; I even got interviewed after the fight. It was about a week later that I met Steve. He seemed pretty cool so we started hanging out. Soon we had started dating. We had only been dating for less than two months when he asked me to marry him. I said yes, but instantly knew I didn't want to. He came to stay with my mom and me while he looked for somewhere to live. Finally after three weeks he decided he was going to move back to his parents' house. The catch to that one was I was supposed to go with him. I didn't want to at all. I was perfectly happy where I was. He complained about it until I finally agreed to go. This was only making a bad situation worse for me, but I thought I would just have to make the best of it. The last straw for me was when he started getting mad about me boxing and doing Jujitsu, which I started doing that summer. He would come down to the gym where I boxed and be a jerk to everybody. Sometimes he would get there before I did and wait for me. I finally decided to leave around the beginning of my junior year in college. I had taken all that I could stand. One day he got mad at me for looking at a newer car that went by. He said that he knew I wanted the driver and I literally thought to myself, "This guy is nuts." That night I called my dad to ask if I could move back home. My dad said yes and I moved back. Steve kept calling me and threatening me to the point I almost had to get a restraining order. The last call I got he was in jail for beating some guy up and it was supposedly my fault because I had left him. I was just like "Oh well, you're a dumbass." I decided to concentrate on school and boxing. At this point in time, I had enough guys to last me a lifetime.

CRITICAL THINKING QUESTIONS

1. How was her background different from most delinquents?
2. Is her life story a reminder that society is better off not giving adolescents a delinquent label?
3. Why did she become involved in drug use?
4. Do you believe that as many high school athletes are involved in drugs as delinquent acts?

I Grew Up In New Orleans

When I was young growing up in New Orleans, the main thing was trying to make it out alive. You were meant to be left there and, as an African American boy, not to make it out alive. You were left there to be institutionalized, in the jail system and in the prison system.

I was an athlete, but even in school teachers never saw you as a person. They only saw you as an athlete, never the student. They would never give you a chance. It got to the point where I didn't give myself a chance. I thought of football and of my friends as an escape.

My mom had two set of twins, all boys. I have a twin brother, and I have two older twin brothers. We lived in a bad neighborhood; in our part of town, it seems like people were being killed each day. I almost got killed, too. My older twin brothers were raising me to play football. I looked up to them, but also in a bad light I saw what they did—from selling drugs, to running women, to using drugs. I picked up on that. I looked up to them so I thought maybe I can do that kind of stuff, too.

My dad was around, but he wasn't around. You could say he had a lot of the ladies of the night around. My mom wasn't the only one who saw this; I saw it for myself. My dad never helped me with my homework. He never even asked if I had homework. He would only ask how the game went that I was playing in. He never even came to see me play football. It was like he was never really ever around. He was there when it was time to go to sleep, and that's was it.

When I was young, I made a lot of runs for drug dealers. I was in elementary school, eight– and nine–years–old making runs for the dealers. I would see those guys; they were ridin' nice, had the women, all the flashy jewelry, and nice cloths. I wanted to have it also and so I made runs. My cousin and uncles know those guys, so that's how I got hooked up. On an average run, I would make about $250.00.

I would go to the corner store. There would be a certain time when they would show up, and I would get some goods and take care of business. Basically, I was a cover up. I would protect those that the police were looking for, so they didn't have to do it.

I never got into using because I was in football, but I did a lot of selling. When I was growing up, I was selling little things, like marijuana, but then I went to selling cocaine and heroin. I needed to make money; my mom worked but she didn't have that much to give me what I wanted, like clothes for school. In high school, you had to be flashy.

So I got caught up in selling drugs and then I got caught. Luckily, it was a cop from my own area, and he gave me a second chance. He took my drugs and brought me to jail, for like an hour and that was it. But I didn't learn my lesson. I wound up going right back to selling. I needed money. That money makes you want to do that. Money is the problem and is the hardest thing to let go of. I got arrested and had a couple ounces of marijuana in my shoes and a couple bags of cocaine. This is what happens when you are in the hood. I needed to make money and that was the quickest way of doing it.

Football was my love. I love doing it, and being out there. Football brought along a lot of the other things, like women. If you are a decent looking football player, women go after you. After the games, we would have like three to five women each. That was part of the fun we would have after the games.

When people I was with robbed people, I took part in it. I was a third party. I didn't actually rob them, but I held the gun. I really had no choice. You know, if the person makes the wrong move, you better squeeze that trigger. I would have had to pull the trigger. If you're from the hood in New Orleans, you're basically family. You can't let nothing happen to a person from your hood.

The first time I saw someone get shot I was like twelve years old. It was two blocks from the university I never looked in the paper, but I think the person might have been a student. The dude gave up the money. I never understood why we shot the dude. The dude made the statement, 'God is not going to bless this,' and we killed him. He got two shots to the head. I looked down and saw the dude's head bleeding. I knew he was dead once he hit the ground. He was done.

After that I got kind of use to seeing it. Cause every other week or every month, dead bodies who had been recently shot were lying in the street. The cops would leave these dead bodies there for two or three hours. But in high school, I saw my best friend get killed. It kind of hit me then. If you don't slow down, this could be you in the street bleeding from your head. Your mom is on her knees trying to pick up your guts.

My best friend and I were coming out of a store, and we heard gun shots outside. We always heard gun shots, but we didn't think these shots were close. Then, they saw us walking out of the store. They jumped out of a car and shot my friend. And luckily for me once I heard the first shot, I ran back into the store and dove over the counter. The owner didn't think I was robbing the place because he had heard the gun shots, too. My best friend had like eight shots in his chest. He splattered like a pump. He had no back to his head. After looking at him like that, I knew I had to get out of New Orleans because I kept thinking another day and that could be me.

A lot of the cops in New Orleans are from New Orleans. So we know their names. And they knew who I was. They knew I wasn't a bad kid, but they knew I wasn't a good kid. There are a lot of dirty cops; they wouldn't bring you to jail. They would take your drugs or money and they would keep it. They wouldn't report it. They would just keep it. You may say it's dirty, but I would say it saves a lot of people by not bringing them to jail.

The most time I have ever spent in jail was two weeks and that was recently when I was in college. I went home for a semester and went to jail for mistaken identity. They thought I was someone else. I did fit the description but I don't understand why it would take two weeks to clear it up. I think they were waiting to see if I was going to snitch on someone. They were basically trying to see what they could get out of me and what I knew.

That was the first time I had spent a night in jail, and I saw people in jail get raped. Luckily, I was from up–town New Orleans, and I knew a lot of the guys I was in jail with. So it really saved my behind. They always want to test a new face, but no one wants to test you if you know guys. Cause if they mess with you, they mess with everyone else. I was in a jail cell with about seventy–five inmates. They were all black men, some of them were killers, and I had never seen so many angry people in my whole life.

I didn't graduate from high school until I was twenty–one years old, cause I didn't do right. Finally I had a professor, a white professor, who showed me the way. He said I always tried, but he also said I tried to do more then I could handle. He sat down and helped me take the ACT. I would have never made it into college if it wasn't for this white professor. Down in New Orleans I didn't like white people and they didn't like me. The reason I let this white professor help me because I respected him. One thing I noticed he treated everyone the same. Can you imagine being in high school at twenty–one years old? It was tough.

CRITICAL THINKING QUESTIONS

1. What effect would it have on a young person to be exposed to so much violence?

2. What rationalization did he use that he needed to continue selling drugs, regardless of the risk?

3. Why do you think he continued to stay in high school, even when he was older than his peers?

4. His life was similar to so many other adolescents growing up in the inner city, other than getting out without spending a major part of his life in juvenile and adult institutions. How did he manage to escape institutionalization?

5. Do you believe that there is the degree of corruption in the New Orleans Police Department suggested by the author of this story?

5

Walking Different Paths

During my childhood, I suppose I walked a different path than most Latino girls. First, I think I was conflicted as far as my sexual preference was concerned. Also, I was a good girl in front of my parents and in school, but outside of that, I was really mischievous. I sneaked out of the house at night and there were a lot of other kids like me where I hung out.

My parents divorced when I was two or three years old. My mother remarried a few years later. In the meantime, I stayed with my grandparents. When my mother remarried, she and my stepdad moved often, but I threw a fit and wanted to stay at the same school. My grandmother let me stay with her so I could still go to the same school, not because my mother couldn't take care of me. I wound up living with my grandmother all the way through high school.

Role Playing

I played the good girl role at school. I would hang out with the nice girls, "the preppie girls." I went to school functions with them, and my parents liked them. The teachers always saw me as real innocent and so I got away with a lot of little things.

However, my bad girl role would sneak out after 10 p.m. or whenever my grandmother would pass out. She was an alcoholic. I would sometimes put her to bed. If I studied, it was always after she passed out.

I guess I was about eleven or twelve when I started to leave home at night. I started hanging around the neighborhood at all hours. I would stay out until it was time to get the last bus home. We were known as the town freaks.

I lived on the wide side of San Antonio, which was predominantly Hispanic or Mexican American. I used to like going to downtown San Antonio. The police didn't have a hold on what was going on downtown, and it was pretty dangerous for a while. When I went downtown, I hung out with the undesirables.

With this group, I did my share of deviant acts. I would drink, smoke pot, and take pills. I don't know what we were taking half the time. Whatever pills they had, we'd try that. I never intentionally did coke, but the other people in the group said I did because it was in a joint. We would also panhandle. We got worse and that's why I eventually decided that I couldn't hang with them anymore.

That wasn't the only thing I did. I would also hang out with some other girls called the "rowdies." They wore dark eyeliner and dark lipstick, and they listened to rock music. They weren't really prostitutes, because they didn't get paid for it, but they would do whatever the boys wanted. They also used a lot of drugs and alcohol.

I took the role as an observer, but I still think it made me an accomplice. I simply hung out with them, but didn't get involved in their sexual stuff.

We spray painted a lot of things, especially boyfriends' cars or houses. But the thing I did the most was steal, and I mostly did it with the group I hung out with at night. They liked purses as well as other things. One time we broke into a pharmacy and they ransacked it. I stayed outside; I was the driver. We sure had a good time partaking in the goodies they got from the drugstore.

My grandmother carried a lot of cash. I would take a twenty–dollar bill or a couple of them. I would use the money for video games. They were really big at the time.

Teenage Pranks

I got caught stealing one time when I was shopping with my grandmother. I liked taking CDs. I took a CD with me and left the store. When we got in the car, security came out. My grandmother was upset, but it wasn't the last time that I got caught stealing when I was with her.

However, when I got caught by my aunt, she really let me have it in Spanish and in English. That's when I stopped stealing because she threatened to tell my mom. My mom used to really beat my butt, and I was afraid of her. Otherwise, if my aunt hadn't caught me, I really don't know what would have happened.

I learned to drive and started to take my grandmother's car in the middle of the night. We laughed about it at the time because she thought her car had a gas leak. My aunt knew about it. She kept warning me that if I took off in that car, something was going to happen. I would say, "I'm careful. I am just going to see my friends."

One night I took the car. We rolled it out of the garage and pushed it as we usually do. I was with my cousin, and we decided to go downtown. I didn't know driving could be so exhausting; there were too many lights. I said I wanted to go back because I was tired. As we pulled up to a traffic light, it went from red to green. A big white car, a caddy, ran the yellow. I didn't see it coming, and "bam," he hit me right in the driver's side.

We weren't hurt, but I thought to myself that my grandmother was going to kill me. And then the "caddy" backed up (I can see the guy's face to this day); he drove around me and took off. We didn't know what to do. We pulled into a parking lot cause all you could hear was the scrapping of metal. The parking lot turned out to be next to the downtown police department. So, here comes an officer, who made me call my home. When I called, my aunt answered; she said she had to call my mom and tell my grandmother. We waited out front.

My aunt and grandmother showed up, and my grandmother started to slap me around in front of the PD. My grandmother kept yelling in Spanish. I kept my head down. My grandmother drove home. I sat in the back. She still somehow succeeded in slapping me a couple times in the car. As soon as we got home, she lectured me until I fell asleep. She was not happy.

While I was busy with the town freaks or with the rowdies, my cousin started dabbling with the Crips and the Bloods. And we wound up having drive–bys at my grandmother's house. There are bullets holes in that house today. But the thing is, I never brought any grief to my home and my cousin did.

Problems at School

My mother, aunt, and grandfather became aware by junior high that I was developing problems at school. They knew I was bad – they just did not know how bad. In junior high, my referral folder had to be at least three inches thick. The school officials always called my mom, and she would get there in 5 minutes. I just got paddled.

I guess the worst thing I did in school, and that I had remorse over, was a beating we gave this one girl. We literally kicked her ass. We beat her so bad that she couldn't get up. We were trying to initiate her into a gang. I was the friend of a member and didn't have to get my ass kicked like that to get into the gang. My venture into gangs did not go beyond junior high.

A number of my friends went to Juvenile Detention, but I never got into the system. I always looked innocent. If I got caught with them, teachers would wonder what I was doing with them. I remember teachers saying, "Melissa, you shouldn't be there." My friends would take the fall for it; they never ratted or anything.

In junior high, although I hung out with the preppie crowd, I would sneak out to the yard at lunch time where everyone else was smoking cigarettes or joints or drinking Nyquil. We couldn't get alcohol so we would drink Nyquil. Everybody kept an eye out in case a teacher came, so that we could destroy or hide whatever we were doing.

I thought it was cool to be in the three groups. My groups at night knew about the preppies, but my little preppie friends didn't know about the groups at night. I did have a problem keeping up with the preppies because they were wearing Esprit and Ferenza, and all these designer clothes I didn't have.

But my sexual identity was the major problem I faced. I always waited to like boys. I remember being in junior high and wondering when I was going to like boys. Then I realized it was not going to happen. I knew I couldn't tell my family. My mom has a cousin who was gay and they gave him a lot of flack for it. I was really afraid to say anything,

I was content with my life of drinking and partying. It certainly didn't discourage me from drinking and smoking when I saw so much of it at home. My grandmother was a heavy drinker, and my stepdad drank a lot, too. Actually, everyone in the family drank. My aunt and grandmother smoked.

In high school, my late hours were getting the best of me. I had my mom on my case when I started getting busted for skipping school. I also had struggles with my sexual identity. My mom told a counselor that I was suicidal. The counselor was the first person I met with a PhD, and I was impressed by the way she talked to me. The way she treated me was different. When she explained to about college, I did a 180 degree shift. She turned me around, turned my tail right around.

I knew I was smart. I had always made good grades, but I really got into school. I really began to like computer math. Slowly but surely, my outside friends started to go by the wayside. I began to hang out with honor students. The counselor was the one who opened my eyes.

I didn't know what college was until my sophomore year in high school. No one in my family, except my mom, ever got a high school diploma. The reason I got into to college was because of my girlfriend's friend. I asked her if she could try to get me into college.

My college education has been in process for some time. I have worked with Americorps. I worked for the city of San Antonio. I worked with the police department and for the Department of Justice. I am currently going to receive a degree in political science, which has a lot to do with 9/11. I do like the study of sociology and law enforcement, and I am considering grad school. I would like to end up with a PhD, but financially, I don't know if I can swing that.

CRITICAL THINKING QUESTIONS

1. How difficult would it be for a young person to be accepted by three diverse social groups during his or her high school years? How did Melissa manage to pull this off?
2. Why was Melissa not discovered in her various deviant encounters?
3. What explanations found in the text would explain, in part, Melissa's drug involvement?
4. What was the major reason Melissa escaped a delinquent label? Did she have a turning point?

6

It Has Been Quite a Ride

Even though there have been many painful, hurtful, and negative events that have occurred in my life, I would not change most of them, because it has made me into a strong independent person. The person that I am today is because of the life I have lived up to this point.

I was born into a family of two loving, married parents. My parents already had a son, who at the time of my birth was seven and a half years old. At this point in time it would have appeared to the outside world as if we were the perfect family, two parents who were together and married, and two children one boy and one girl. Just because it looks good on the surface, doesn't mean it is good on the inside.

Going up as a child, I spent my early years at home with my mother. I never attended daycare or went to a babysitter growing up because my mother was a stay at home mom. We would spend our days tending to the house and going shopping. My brother had to go to school of course, but there were those days he would stay at home and spend the day with mom and me. My father worked full–time as a construction worker. I do not remember seeing my father home very much, growing up as a child. My mother was my best friend my entire life, I always wanted to be just like her. She spent all of her time with my brother and me, no matter how much trouble we got in she would always be on our side.

My father built me my very own sandbox in the backyard. He also taught me how to ride my first bike. And later came riding the bike without training wheels. Prior to me beginning school my father spent weekends with me. We would go to the park and go fishing. As I grew older, it seemed as if my father grew more and more distant from our family. I thought it was because he had to work so much. Little did I know at that time his cocaine addiction was getting worse and was beginning to change his priorities.

At the age of five is when I began to realize my perfect world was not as perfect as I had thought it to be. I remember waking up in the middle of the night to crying, yelling, and screaming. I remember standing in the doorway of my parent's room waiting to see if my father was going to hit my mom, and the second he did I was going to run and call 911. I didn't want anyone to hurt my mother; in my eyes she was the most beautiful nicest woman you would ever meet. My dad always treated her like shit and she didn't deserve it. He was the one lying, cheating, and using drugs, where mom spent her time with my brother and me. As the fighting and the hitting began to get worse and worse, I began to spend a lot more time staying with my mother's parents.

The violence in my family by the time I began preschool had reached an all time high. I will never forget the night my mom was trying to leave my father. She had called her friend and explained that life had got to the point that she couldn't stay with him anymore. Prior to this night, my mom was constantly seen with black eyes and bruises all over her face. While I was waiting in the car packed and ready to go with mom and her friend, she realized she had forgotten something in her car. My mom went back to the garage and got in her station wagon in the backseat to get what she had forgotten. My father heard her from inside of the house and came out and beat the shit out of her to try and stop her from leaving. I remember all I could see was the station wagon moving up and down from the blows from mother was taking to her face. Her friend called the cops, and they were there within ten minutes. I rode to the hospital with my mother holding her hand and crying like a baby.

I never understood why he was so mean to her, she didn't deserve it. I loved my mother and I hated seeing her unhappy and hurt. I spent the night by the side of my mother's bed, and in the morning my father came and brought her flowers and said he was sorry. I never understood why she always forgave him, maybe it was love or maybe it was because she knew that it was the drugs making him that way, and he used to be a caring gentle man. I will never forget the pain he caused my mother, and a part of me will never forgive him for that. I never second guessed my mother's decisions, but it tore me apart watching her cry day after day. Yet she always stayed, I never understood. If I was her I would have left. To me it makes no sense, that's why I promised myself and my brother that I would never let a man do that to me.

During my kindergarten years, I enjoyed and looked forward to going to school, maybe that was because I didn't want to be at home. Things changed though when my father was arrested. There was a big drug bust; there were about ten people involved. Of the ten, my father was one of them; for the first time he was at the wrong place at the wrong time. My father was one of them that ended up getting convicted and sentenced to serve ten years in prison on a drug charge. I spent the remainder of my kindergarten year and my first grade year visiting my father in prison. I remember telling everyone that during the weekend we visited my father in prison.

When my father was in prison, he wrote to the family. He always told us he missed us and things would be better when he came home. Everything sounds good on paper though, that doesn't always mean it will be the same when they come home. My father only spent two years in prison, because he was paroled for good behavior. When my father came home, we had a huge party for him at the house, with all of our friends and family. My mother always said to me, "the man that went to prison is not the same as the man that came home."

When I was six I was still unclear what that meant, as the time went by I began to realize what my mother meant. Spending two years of your life in prison is an experience you would hope would change someone for the better, however; that is not always the case. My father returned home and continued his habits as normal. He began using cocaine again. My mom was right, the man that left returned home, but he was no longer the same man. He began spending all of his time and money on himself. My father had a custom built motorcycle that was blue with flames; my mom called it the "blue whore." He spent all of his time cheating on my mother and when he did finally come home, there was always fights that lead to more violence.

After dad was released from prison, my brother began to act more and more like our father. He began using drugs and getting into a lot of trouble. If he wasn't getting kicked out of school, he was always skipping. Kevin began to steal a lot. He stole money, drugs, car stereos, clothes and items from the mall, basically anything that appealed to him. The problem with my brother is he was never very good at being a criminal, he was always getting caught!!

When I was in third grade, at the age of eight, I got into my first fight at school. Gym class had just gotten over, and we were standing in line by the door. We were all talking about the flag football game we had just played. I was the team captain for my team, and another girl was the team captain for the other team. She and I had never gotten

41

along; she was the rich snobby girl that thought she knew everything. I was the girl who didn't care about what people thought, so I said whatever was on my mind. While we were waiting in line for our third grade teacher to come and pick us up from the gym, she and I got into an argument over which team had won the flag football game. I claimed mine did and she claimed her team did, truth be told it was my team that won the game. She and I argued for about five minutes over it, and then she pushed me into the wall, so I hit her a few times in the face. She bit me, and then ran at me. When she ran at me, I bent over and she flipped over me. The gym teacher came running, our third grade teacher was just walking in the door, and all the kids were cheering. She and I got taken to the principal's office where they called our mothers. Our mothers arrived, and the four of us had to go into the principal's office and talk with the principal. Neither one of us got into trouble; it was just a matter of basically say sorry and don't do it again. That was the end of it, however later in life, and I didn't know when, I intended to get revenge.

Middle school is when my life began to become dramatic. I had spent the earlier years in life seeing everything my brother was doing wrong and basically idolizing him. I saw him get into trouble with the law and I saw him do a great amount of drugs. I thought all that was cool because he was doing it. At the age of eleven, I began smoking weed on a weekly basis. I began to hang out with more people in a nearby larger city. I would spend my weekends with my friends and brother in this city. My parents allowed me to go spend the weekends staying with my brother at his apartment. What began as a weekend thing, to go walk around this city with my friends, turned into a daily period of getting high.

My family life at home began to turn into a constant fight. My father was always yelling at me that I was turning into my brother and that I wasn't going to end up to be anything in life. Well, that didn't really seem like a good argument for him seems how we learned it from him. My father got mad when I would tell him that he raised us this way and we were only turning into what he showed us to become.

My mom and I were still really close, I think she knew that I was doing drugs and stealing car stereos, however, I never admitted it to her. She used drugs, but didn't want me to use them. I was too ashamed to ever tell her that I wasn't the sweet little angel she wanted me to be.

I was still doing well in school, until about the middle of my sixth grade year, when I got into a lot of trouble. Well, one day while I was at school, the same girl I got into a fight with during third grade was running her mouth about me and saying how I wasn't any good in basketball. Everyone in the hallway was around and everyone was cheering for us to fight. Instead of doing the smart thing and letting it go, I hit her, I got in a few quick punches before the teachers came and broke it up. When we got to the principal's office Dana started crying and blaming it all on me, I started it she said. She made it look like she was the victim, which looking back now she was.

The other girl got sent to the nurse to have her face looked at and was then sent back to class. However, I had to sit and get yelled at by the principal while I waited for my mom to get there. Once my mother arrived, the principal told my mom that I was being suspended from school for a week because I got into a fight. My mother got into an argument with the principal because she did not believe it was fair that I was the only one being punished. The principal told my mother that other students have reported me harassing them, and there was more students than just Dana that were scared of me. Therefore he felt this would be the best way to let me cool off and clear my head.

I started to go through a period in my life where my self–esteem was low. I have never seen myself as good enough and I began to go through a phase of cutting. I was so unhappy, and I never was able to express myself or explain why. The only time I was happy was when I was getting into fights, which made me feel free for some reason. My fighting got worse, but as the fighting got worse, so did the cutting. I would take a razor blade and cut all the way up and down my arms, inside and out. At first no one knew about it, but it became obvious when during the spring time of my sixth grade year I was always wearing long sleeves.

One morning when I was in the shower, my mom walked in and saw my arms; she started yelling and crying asking me why I would do something like that to myself. I told her I didn't know why I did it. She told me to finish my shower and get dressed she was going to take me and get me help. My mom took me to our family doctor, where we all three sat down and talked about what was bothering me. They decided that I needed to speak with a child psychologist and that I needed to be on antidepressants. My mother went with me to meet with the psychologist; I only met with her twice, before I decided I never wanted to go back.

I was not and still am not comfortable opening up and talking to people. My entire life my brother always told me "Keep a wall up, trust no one, trust will get you hurt." I have stuck by that. I never wanted to talk to the psychologist and I never did open up. My mother and I sat down after my second visit with the psychologist. She told me I didn't have to go, but that she thought it would be a good idea for me to keep a journal. A journal, she told me, could be my way of letting everything out and I would never had to show it to anyone. I agreed to do the journal thing as long as I didn't have to go back to the psychologist. I took the antidepressants for about two months, before I stopped taking them. They were not helping me at all; in fact the doctor said he believed they were making me more violent.

I continued cutting myself all the way through my sixth grade year. My favorite sport every since I was a young child has been and will always be softball. I realized once softball began how messed up my arms looked. During softball season, I couldn't hide the scars and cut marks. My father agreed to get me laser surgery, because I was too ashamed of what I had done to myself. I had to go through half of softball season with the scars on my arms, and the remainder of the season with it all wrapped due to my surgery.

After my laser surgery I began to feel better about myself, I didn't like having to hide my arms from people; it was embarrassing. During softball season, I was unable to hide it, therefore; my mother told everyone I was experiencing some problems that I am now willing to work through. No one ever bad mouthed me, because ever since I was a child, I was the star softball player. Everyone was more worried about if I would be able to play than what I had done to my arms.

By eighth grade, I picked up another habit, meth. I wouldn't say I was addicted right away, the first few months I just did it whenever I was with my first boyfriend. After I had been with him for six months, we decided that we wanted to take our relationship to the next level, so we did. I lost my virginity at the age of thirteen, about five months later we broke up

My freshman year of high school was when my drug use skyrocketed. During freshman year is when I began to experiment with other drugs. I tried acid, mushrooms, ecstasy, cocaine and meth. Meth became my favorite. I enjoyed having energy and feeling like I could do anything, to me at that time there was not a better feeling. I would smoke every morning, go to school, come home at lunch to smoke again, go back to school, go to practice, and then come home smoke again and go hang out with my friends. I always hated the nasty dip taste you got in the back of your mouth and the days where all you did was stay in bed and sleep, but for some reason I enjoyed using meth. On the other hand, I was disappointed with cocaine. I didn't like that it didn't give me the energy and motivation that meth did. I was a casual user of cocaine; basically I did it socially, especially when we were in Chicago. Acid was fun! I remember seeing some weird shit, and the first time I tried it I thought I was going to die.

The summer before my sophomore year is when my life ended and my heart died. It was a typically August day, and my mother and I had gotten into a fight. I don't even remember what the fight was about but I do remember telling her "I wish you would die". I never in a million years meant it, nor did I ever in my lifetime want that to happen. However, in the heat of an argument, words just pop out of my mouth. This has always been a characteristic of me. I left my parents house and went to my brother's house to baby–sit my niece and my nephew. My brother was currently in jail, I don't remember for what because he spent most of his life from fifteen on in jail, so I was used to it by now. My sister–in–law Jill was working full time.

This day was a special day at first, because for the first time since my grandfather died my father had talked my mom into going for a motorcycle ride. They stopped at my brother's house and told me goodbye and that they were going on a Harley ride. I kissed and hugged my mother and told her I loved her. When they walked out that door, I never in my life would have believed what would happen next. At 5:15 PM, while my parents were traveling northbound, a car turned in front of them. My mother was thrown from the bike, and my father held on for his life to the handle bars. The ironic thing was that at the stop sign at the exact same intersection watching a car turn in front of my parent's motorcycle was my dad's best friend.

This is the part where my life ends… my heart breaks… and my life and myself will never be the same again. Shortly after 5:15 PM, my dad's best friend Doug showed up at the doorstep of my brother's house. He was covered in blood and he was crying. He

45

told me that my parents had been in a car accident and that it didn't look good. I didn't start crying at first because to me it was a dream. I was so scared, confused, worried, and most of all in shock. On the way to the hospital, we passed the scene of the accident. I remember I was crying and in my mind I kept thinking this can't be true, it isn't them. As we passed the accident scene, I saw my father's custom built motorcycle on the ground in pieces. I saw white sheets on the road, and blood all over the place. I also saw the car and the son–of–a bitch that killed my mother. I began to scream and cry in the car yelling that it can't be. Why would this happen to me? I arrived at the hospital just in time to say goodbye to my father. His injuries were serious and life threatening, however; they believed that he would be able to receive better medical attention at Mayo Clinic in Rochester, Minnesota. They said that he was strong enough and they believed it would not threaten his life to take the flight. I kissed my father's forehead and told him I would see him soon. I remember looking at my dad and seeing his bones through his arms, because the skin was completely gone. I then went into the waiting room and waited for the doctor to come in and talk to me. The nurse had told me my mother was in surgery because she had internal bleeding that they needed to get it stopped. As I sat in the waiting room, the room began to fill with family and friends. The only person that wasn't there and the only person that I wanted and needed there was my brother. I called the jail and explained to them what had happened to my parents and I needed my brother. The judge agreed to release my brother. In fact they not only released him, they had a deputy bring him to the hospital, and he never had to go back to finish his sentence.

My brother finally arrived after an hour or so, just as the doctor was coming in to talk to me. My brother and I were told by the doctor, that mom had suffered numerous injuries. She had internal bleeding, brain damage, and had broken bones, and she would not survive through the night. The doctor told us that we should go in and be with her and say our goodbyes; he said that she could hear us but couldn't respond. I went into the hospital room, and there was my mother lying on a hospital bed dying. I never in my life felt so helpless. I remember looking at her and her face and head were swollen. The only visible cut she had was right above her left eye on her forehead and it was about an inch long. My brother was scared; he was crying; he didn't want to look at mom. I never understood then but I do now. He doesn't remember mom with the swollen face and I do.

He remembers mom as the beautiful women that she was; he never did look at her. He went up and kissed her forehead and touched her hand but he either kept his eyes closed or his head down. I remember looking at the cut on her forehead and thinking she's not hurt bad, she can make it. It was wishful thinking though my brother left the room after saying his goodbyes.

I never left. I stayed by my mother's side holding her hand, I begged her to come back to me. I didn't want to lose my mom. I felt so helpless staring at her in pain and dying knowing there was nothing that I could do. I prayed to God to bring my mother back, and I also prayed to take me, not her. My mother was a caring loving person. She would help anyone with anything; she would of given the shirt off her back if someone had asked her. On the other hand, I am a heartless, selfish bitch, if anyone deserved to die it was me. I stayed by my mother's side the entire night, holding her hand, rubbing her hair with my hand, and kissing her forehead and hand. I begged, and begged, and begged her to come back to me. I loved my mom. Life without her is something I never wanted to experience. To sit in a room and hold her hand, knowing I couldn't help her tore me apart, it ripped my heart out, I always wanted to be there for my mother, and for the first time in my life I couldn't help her. I sat by her side, and cried, and cried. I kept talking to her, telling her how much I needed her, how much I loved her, and that I couldn't live without her. I'm not sure if she heard me, the doctor says she could, but to this very day I pray that she heard me so she knows how much I truly love her.

At 1:00 AM the doctor returned to the room. The doctor explained to us how the impact of mom hitting the ground had caused major brain damage. He told us that her brain had stopped working, and her heart would quit anytime now. Friends of the family came in and said their goodbyes. My brother and his wife said their goodbyes, and I sat in the room with her until 3:14 AM when my mother's heart stopped beating and she died.

I stayed in the room with my head on her lap, balling my eyes out. My best friend, my mother, her life all had just come to an end. After about ten minutes I got up, kissed my mom goodbye, told her I loved her, and how sorry I was, and left the room. Before I left the hospital, the nurses handed me three bags of belongings. One bag had my father's leather coat and pants in it, covered in blood. The other bag had my mother's leather coat and pants in it, covered in blood and cut from being cut off of her. And the third bag, the nurse told me to go in the bathroom and flush, it was my father's drugs. The nurse informed me that she won't tell the police, but if I leave with the drugs and get pulled over I would be charged. I took the bags, went into the bathroom, and then came back out. There was over three thousand dollars worth of glass in that bag that had come from my father's boot; there was no way I was going to flush that much shit. I left the bathroom and left the hospital.

The car ride home for me was a blur. I don't remember anything except sitting there in complete shock holding my mother's leather coat. I still had tears rolling down my face, and it was as if my body was physically alive, but the rest of me was dead. I went home; we all showered and changed, and got back into the car and drove to Rochester Minnesota, to the hospital where dad was.

When I arrived at the hospital, they handed me a whole bunch of forms with various questions in regards to my father's medical history. I filled the forms out and I remember that the one question I didn't know whether to tell the truth or lie was "Does your father use illegal street drugs?" The answer was yes, but I lied and checked no. They told me that my father's surgery had been successful. My father had numerous injuries: his pelvic bone was broken in three places, his arms were completely messed up and broken, and he was on a breathing tube so he was unable to talk. His arms had to have bone grafts, skin grafts, and metal pins put into them. The injuries on his arms would take months, years to heal, and once my father recovered, he would have to learn how to walk, eat, and move around by himself all over again.

The day of the funeral was a living hell. To begin the morning, my brother Kevin refused to go to the funeral, finally after fighting and crying we got him convinced that he needed to be there. When I finally did arrive at the church, I was informed that the person who had killed my mother had sent flowers. I demanded that those flowers be thrown away immediately. Then I was asked if I wanted the coffin open or closed. I decided that I wanted it closed, because my mother was a beautiful petite woman and the woman in the coffin was swollen and didn't look like her. I wanted everyone to remember mom the way my brother got to, perfect, not the way I remember.

And I had to deal with the fact that my mother's sister showed up drunk to the funeral. My mother was so ashamed and embarrassed when she had shown up at their father's funeral drunk; I refused to allow her to do it at my mother's funeral, too. My aunt was outside with her new boyfriend, and they were smoking; I walked outside and didn't say anything, just started punching her in the face. I hit her numerous times over and over in the face before they pulled me off of her. Once they removed me from her, I told her she was not welcome here and she had to leave. She refused to go; therefore, my brother told her the same thing. He threatened to have them let go of me and I'd continue to beat her until she left. Finally she got the hint and left.

Later on, I will never forget one day when my dad and I were sitting in his hospital room talking. He told me he was sorry for my mom, sorry for how bad my childhood had been, and that he was going to make it up to me. We had an understanding finally between the two of us, I knew he was all I had and he knew I was all he had. My father told me once he was released from the hospital he was going to improve our lives, he was going to quit using drugs and he was also going to quit selling drugs, just like he wrote from prison.

When I was staying at my parent's house, my friend and I were getting drunk or smoking glass all the time. We had parties every night we were there. I will never forget one day my friend and I showed up at school for English class; we had just got high and had been drinking. She had done drugs before, but glass was new to most people and was messing them up worse than they were used to. My brother and I always joked about how drugs ran in our veins and that's why stronger drugs didn't affect us and turn us out like it had done to most people. Our English teacher came up and asked how we were doing, and my friend started crying and yelling "Stop yelling at us." We were sent home. I passed all of my classes that year and no one could understand how I did it when I was there once or twice a week, if that.

After losing my mom, I attempted suicide five times. I cut my wrists three times and tried to overdose the other two times. I was hospitalized two times; both times they made me drink this nasty charcoal stuff to clean my system out. My take on life was without my mom I didn't want to be alive anymore.

By the end of my sophomore year of high school, my father had made a fairly well recovery. He didn't have full use of his arms, but he never will. My father and I developed a relationship together, but we couldn't live together because we fought too much. My father had broken his promise about quitting; he was still using and selling drugs just as much now as he was before.

In May 2002, I graduated from high school. After graduation, one of my girlfriend's dad came up to me and told me that my mother would be very proud of me. I started crying, because I knew she would not be happy about me smoking or selling drugs; in fact she would be disappointed. My mother always wanted me to be the one that got away and did something with my life and not end up like the rest of my family. She loved my brother but she didn't want me to be like him in and out of trouble and jail.

After graduation, that was the day that I changed my life. I wanted to make my mother proud, I decided to quit selling and using drugs, and I did. I just stopped——no rehabilitation, no nothing. I was a bitch, but I took my aggression out in fighting. Every time I felt that I needed a pick me up I would fight that much harder or train that much harder. I wanted to be better than what I had become. I wanted to make something of myself.

Currently, I am ready to graduate from college. However, the last four years have not been easy. I got married, and my husband, like my father and brother, got into selling drugs and is now finishing a prison sentence. My brother has been in and out of prison, and my father is now in federal court and will likely receive a long prison sentence. I do have a beautiful daughter. I have raised our daughter by myself since my husband has been incarcerated. But she goes to visit him, talks to him, and she knows who he is. I have been drug free for four years and five months now. I am used to life being hard and full of obstacles though, so I will handle whatever life hands me next!

CRITICAL THINKING QUESTIONS

1. What experiences did this person have that made her life so difficult?
2. Why did the author of this story quit using drugs?
3. Why did her brother and father continue to use and sell drugs in spite of the mounting costs?
4. What challenges does the author of this story face in the future?
5. Ultimately, why has she prevailed in the midst of what seemed to be overwhelming problems?

7

From Gang Member to College Football Star

The following is a verse from a rap I wrote, entitled "Appreciate:"

> 1979 was the scene was a dream broke, the
>
> scene when a dream gave a black queen more hope.
>
> A seventeen–year–old, honor role,
>
> college hopeful devastated found out she was
>
> impregnated. She can now say goodbye to
>
> those college dreams, goodbye to those better
>
> things, hello to baby's cries and screams.
>
> Plus she knew her parents wouldn't approve.
>
> What else could she do, left with only one
>
> choice to choose? Abortion was the only move
>
> that seemed realistic, 'cause no way she was
>
> going to end up another statistic. That was
>
> her reasoning, ends justify the means, but
>
> the night before she had a dream. Of better
>
> things to come, and victories won, and how
>
> one day she was to birth a son. And he
>
> would be great, and I appreciate God
>
> for putting that in her mind state.

At the age of seventeen, my mom was a straight–A student and a member of the National Honor Society. She was the second oldest of four sisters and two brothers. She was also the best–behaved of her siblings. The oldest was her sister Mary, named after my great–grandmother. Besides being the eldest of the siblings, Mary was the most intelligent, had more street smarts, and was the worst behaved. Mary could always be expected to be getting into some sort of trouble and do anything and everything for her siblings.

When my mother first found out she was pregnant, it just seemed right that the two of them would concoct a plan to have Mary say the child was hers after my mom gave birth. When they realized that their plan was flawed, my mother then considered abortion. She tells me now that the only reason she did not go through with it was because she had a dream that she would have a great son. This decision to have me was hard for my mom because she was always the one expected to go to college and become the family's great success story. She was also embarrassed because she knew that her parents would be disappointed. There was no telling what accomplishments would be lost to her forever by giving birth to me.

> Same year, different tears, this time for
> joy instead of fear. Almost didn't make it
> but I finally here, butt naked 8 pounds, 7
> ounces when the doctor spanked my rear.
> That wouldn't be the last time that would
> happen, a little bad ass in class that loved
> yappin', loved scrappin', loved rappin'. It
> seemed my mom loved tappin' my back end,
> 'cause back then I deserved it. All them
> messages she was yellin', hell yeah I heard it,
> that shit hurted, but now I see it was worth
> it. And thanks for holding on to those
> college dreams, because you pushed on, and
> stayed strong you provided us with better
> things. You got your degree when others said
> you couldn't, when others said you wouldn't,
> even some said you shouldn't. But you
> showed them and showed me that all things
> are possible through God when you believe.

So I was finally out to wreak havoc on the world. One of the first orders of business was to move from Cleveland, Ohio to Englewood, California at the age of two with my mom. She moved there to go to a community college and live with her cousins. After a few years there, we moved back to Cleveland, Ohio. She then attended Cuyahoga Community College to become an X–ray technician.

In the meantime, I was at home playing with my newfound cousin, Chantea. It seems that while in the Army, stationed in Florida, my Aunt Mary decided to pick up somebody for me to play with, literally. Chantea was one year older than me and brought back to Cleveland under the guise of Mary's daughter. I later found out that Juan, a well–known Florida drug dealer, and Mary had kidnapped Chantea from Juan's ex who had severely abused her. Chantea arrived in Cleveland with severe burns on the left side of her body, along with scattered cigarette burns.

Now there were ten of us living in one house, including my grandmother, my grandfather, my mom, my cousin Chantea, and myself. Chantea and myself were prone to get into trouble in school, although I had straight A's.

After three years of getting spanked seemingly every day, something happened that, as I look back, was a critical day in my life. It started as just another day in second grade with my old white teacher, Mrs. Something–or–Other, telling me that I was in trouble for throwing something across the class. I was not going to let her get the last word, especially since I didn't do it. I think I was tired of getting a spanking every day. Something started to grow inside of me that day. It felt like heat, but not a warm external heat; it was a hot heat that started in the depths of my stomach and grew in size and moved higher up with every comment I said to the teacher, proclaiming that I hadn't done anything. She told me to come to the front of the class. As I stood up and started to walk toward her, I could feet the heat hit my throat and increase in intensity at every word that came out of her mouth about how bad I was going to get it. When I reached her, she grabbed me, and the heat took control and I hit her. I was sent to the office and paddled. My mom then went up to the school to meet with the teacher. According to my mother, the teacher was so drunk that she could hardly answer me. Because of this, my mom decided to take me out of the public schools and sent me to St. Joseph.

St. Joseph was on St. Clair Boulevard, one of the worst places in Cleveland. I transferred in the middle of my second–grade year. I tested so high that the nuns wanted to move me up a grade level. My grandfather didn't let that happen.

One side of St. Clair was known as the 4 Block. The 4 Block was a Blood hood. Right across the street was the Crip hood. My great–grandmother lived across the corner in the Crip hood. I stayed there most of the time because I could walk to school and back. I learned a lot in third grade at that school. Most lessons were related to the streets though.

Collinswood High School was two blocks down the street from our school, and the high school kids walked by our school everyday to go home. All of the Bloods and Crips from the neighborhood went to that school, and they would fight every other day.

One day after school, there was a fight between one of the Bloods from Collinswood and one of the eighth graders from my school. Rob beat that guy so bad that I don't know to this day if he made it. After Rob was sure there was no chance of the other guy getting up, he gave the knuckles back to his friend, who hid them by the sign in front of the school.

The police came and my best friend at the time and I were standing around. One of the officers asked me if I saw where the weapon went. When I started to answer, Frank stepped on my foot and told the officer that we hadn't seen any weapons. Later on Frank explained to me that telling on anyone was never to be done. That lesson has stuck with me to the present, and I have never broken it. That rule plays an important role in my character, and I can't stand anyone who breaks that rule.

Frank lived on the other side of St. Clair, the Blood hood. Most Bloods over there were Betas, which was the name of a street. My great–grandmother's house was on the other side of St. Clair, in the Crip hood across from Delta Park. They referred to themselves as Delta, or Delta Shotgun Crip Gangsters. Nike was another Crip set in the area.

Spending most of my time in the park, I naturally became friends with the Delta set. I was impressed when I would notice their meetings. I used to think that there were so many of them, and they were so organized. Eventually around fifth grade, they wanted me to join. They told me that because I was not originally from their hood, I had to get initiated in. I had to fight this other Crip named Dee for two minutes and get hit from the back by this older guy named Sam. It wasn't too bad. After I was in, I felt like I was a part of their family. They would look out for me all the time.

Shortly after that, I saw somebody get killed for the first time. I was in the park with some of the other younger set members when we heard Barn, an older set member, his sister, and his mother arguing with some guy. Three other Crips came along. The guy began to run. Barn got into his car and ran him down. He got out of the car and killed him. We all started smashing the windows of the victim's car and jumping on it. It didn't really affect me to see that happen. I don't know why, but it just didn't. Bam got sent to jail for murder.

The first time that I ever got a gun pulled on me happened at this same time. I was around the corner from the park at a store. Another Crip came up to me and asked me whether I was holding anything for Sam, the oldest Crip in my set. I knew this guy was a Nike because I used to see him at the park running his mouth. When I told him no, he pulled out this little black revolver. I still can remember it as if it happened yesterday. He told me to empty out my pockets and then he checked my socks. He knew I was a Delta, but I guess he did not care since I was so young. After he realized that I didn't have anything but two dollars, he pushed me and walked off. The funny thing is that I was not even a little bit scared. It was like I knew that if he shot me, he was going to get it next, even though I might be dead. I later told Sam about what happened, and he confronted the dude. The dude denied it all, but Sam believed me and beat him all the way to his block. I never saw him in the park again.

That year in fifth grade at St. Joseph, I got my first grade lower than a B; I got an F. In addition to me continually getting into fights at school, my grades were starting to decline. My mom at the time was looking for a house so we could move out of my grandparents' house. We moved to Euclid, and she transferred me into the Euclid public schools. It was the first time that I had white kids in school with me. At the time we moved in, Euclid was experiencing white flight. During our first year there, the street went from half white to only three white houses on the street.

Euclid schools were experiencing gang activity, but they were in denial that gangs existed. Euclid schools also introduced me for the first time to Folks and Vice Lords. The

Folks became an even more important part of my life in seventh and eighth grade. It seemed that there were no Crips and Bloods in Euclid. Euclid had mostly Folks. I became their friend, and I received respect because of my fighting reputation and because I was a Crip. I learned their lit [literature] and their handshakes, and they even let me come to some of their in–school initiations, but they never let me go to a meeting.

I was impressed that they were more organized and that their lit was more intricate than the Crips. I also saw big money come into the picture. After one dance in eighth grade, the Folks and I walked to McDonald's. On the way there, this old black Chevy with tinted windows pulled up to us and started trippin' [mouthing off]. They were from Valley Low, which is affiliated with the Vice Lords. When we ran up on them, they sped off. About four minutes later they came back shooting. Nobody got hit, but it was the first time I ever got shot at.

I also started going out to clubs in eighth grade, but, of course, my mom never knew. I would spend the night at my older cousins' house, and they would take me out with them. That is also the time when shootings became a regular thing. I also started smoking weed and drinking.

My grades were horrible at Euclid. The principal there was one of the biggest racists I have ever met. I had one good quarter there, because he told me that I couldn't make the honor role if my life depended on it. He also told me that I was nothing and that no matter what, I would never amount to anything. My mom hated him, and she decided that she didn't want me to go to Euclid High the next year.

My mom put in an application to Benedictine High School, a private Catholic school. As usual, I received excellent scores on the admissions testing and was allowed to enroll. I also won a scholarship raffle that lowered my tuition. When my eighth grade principal found out I got accepted, he told me that I wouldn't make it through the first year. He was almost right.

Although Benedictine was a traditionally prestigious high school, it was right dead smack in the middle of the hood. The school was located right on the corner of Martin Luther King, Jr. and Buckeye Drives. A long time ago, it had been a white neighborhood, but white flight had left this a neglected area.

The population of the school was largely black, because white parents no longer wanted to send their kids to school in the middle of the ghetto. It was no surprise to me that there was gang activity again staring me in the face. This time there were Folks, Crips, and a few Vice Lords present in the school. I got into so many fights that year that I could not count them all if I tried. I felt powerful because everyone knew me, and I wanted others to know what would happen if they messed with me.

During my first year at Benedictine, my gang activity was at an all–time high. From fighting to shooting to throwing cocktail bombs at rival gang turf, there was no limit to the mayhem I was involved in. They called me "Da Villain." Blue from the shoes up was my everyday apparel. If I saw somebody with some red laces or hat banged the wrong way, I was on them quick. I would say, "Wuz up Cuz!" Let them say wrong shit, and they were in for some real shit. I have friends that I will never be able to see or talk to again, because they were killed. I didn't want my life to end up like my friends.

The only thing besides gangs that interested me was football. I had been playing organized football since fifth grade. After one of my many fights toward the end of my ninth–grade year, I was once again sent to Mr. Russ's office, the dean of men. That's when he sat down with me and told me that I might not be invited back next year. He told me that I was one of the most athletically gifted students he had seen in quite a while. Something about that talk sunk in, and I began to pull my grades up.

After being invited back my sophomore year, my grades came up even more. I still got into an occasional scrap, but nothing like my freshman year. Mr. Russ and I developed a relationship, based on respect and trust. It also helped me that a lot of my gang friends were kicked out of school.

There was a student organization at Benedictine named the B.C.O. [Black Cultural Organization]. The mediator of the B.C.O. was quitting because he felt like there were people in the hierarchy skimming money. The new mediator opened up the positions of president and all lower positions to sophomores for the first time in the history of the B.C.O. Of course, I took full advantage of the opportunity and became the first underclassman voted president of the B.C.O.

The last president and staff left me with only $85 in the treasury to work with, but that wasn't a problem considering that I now had the title of B.C.O. president behind my name. I went to work and before long, I had over $9,000 in the treasury. Unlike the corrupt presidents of old, I didn't skim from the money earned at school parties. I simply threw non–school–affiliated parties, using the name B.C.O. as a marketing tool. That way, my staff and I could get paid, and we could still build up the B.C.O. treasury.

In my junior year, the vice president and I were two of the founders of an organization we named "the Clan." The Clan was a money–making organization. It included different gang members, cops, and some local record companies. The cops would rob drug dealers instead of arresting them. They would give the drugs to us to sell for a percentage of the profits. We would throw parties to sell the drugs with the police as security. Record companies would pay us to play their groups at their parties and have them perform. We would also get a percentage of the records sold at the parties. It was all about money. There was no gang conflict inside the Clan, even though four gangs were represented, because everyone was making money. The cops were especially making money. Everyone was happy.

The B.C.O. and Clan activities ended with quite a bang. In my senior year at the biggest B.C.O. party in the history of the B.C.O., a fight broke out between some rival gangs from across town. Usually the B.C.O. was able to stop any fights, but the party was so big that nobody could get organized. The fight turned into a shooting, and the B.C.O. was shut down for the year. The Clan still exists in Cleveland, and I continue to consider myself a Clansman. With all the money we made for the B.C.O., we started an annual scholarship fund that still exists today.

My senior year we won state championships in football, track, and basketball. I won all kinds of awards for my football abilities. I had settled down a lot by this time, and I got good grades. College recruiters visited me, and I finally chose one college.

Well, here I am a senior in college. I blew my knee out last year and can't play football anymore. But I am determined to finish college and have only a few courses to go. I think I am going to make the Dean's List this semester. I wish I could see my eighth–grade principal now!

CRITICAL THINKING QUESTIONS

1. Why do you believe that this inner–city gang member turned his life around?

2. How typical do you believe his life was of the average inner–city gang member?

3. Do you believe that the police and this cultural organization worked together to sell drugs?

4. What type of police officer do you believe would participate in such corrupt activities?

5. How much do you think his mother's determination to finish college influenced this individual once his football career ended?

8

She's Just a Party Animal

I wasn't what people would normally think of as a delinquent. I am a middle–class, Caucasian female. I grew up in a small, rural, Iowa town. In high school I had decent grades. My parents were divorced, but I had a stable home life. My parents got divorced when I was two years old. My mother got remarried to my stepfather when I was three. My stepfather is a wonderful person and he accepted me like I was his own child. My father was around when I was a child. I remember spending every other weekend with him and my grandparents.

There wasn't really anything you could say that made me do the things that I did. My childhood was normal, but things started going downhill as I got older. I guess you would say that I had two separate lives. In school no one knew what I was really like. I just had this image that I could do no wrong. I got along with all of the adults. I was pictured as a good kid. My friends in the neighboring town knew better than that. They saw a side of me that my friends at school never saw.

It all started when I was fourteen. I started smoking cigarettes and finding people who were like me. These were people who you would think would never get into trouble until you got to know them. I managed to stay out of trouble until I was sixteen. That was when it all began. That fall I met a girl, Mandy, and my life changed. She had been in trouble before and I was meeting her friends. We would go into the neighboring town of Newton and hang out with friends. I was drinking and smoking cigarettes more than I had before. Just after Thanksgiving I met her brother. He just got out of jail for burglary. Tony and I started talking and we got along great. He was unlike any person that I had ever met before.

There was a lot of attraction between us. We just flirted because we were dating other people. My parents told me to stay away from him, but Mandy was my best friend, so I always had a reason to go over there. During that time I was hanging out with friends and partying. When I was in school I was quiet and reserved, but I felt like myself when I was in Newton.

Tony and I started dating in April. He was sent to a correctional facility in a larger city. It hurt so much to see him leave. He had furloughs to a friend's house and I would go there to see him. I lied to my parents about where I was going. I never told them I was going to see Tony. I would have been in so much trouble if they had found out. During one of his furloughs, I met his friend Rich and they smoked weed. As good as it smelled, I declined smoking it. A couple of days later some friends and I stopped over at Rich's house. It was there that I smoked my first bowl. I liked it a lot. I didn't tell anyone at school. It just wasn't their thing to do.

The next weekend I went with Tony and some friends' back over to Rich's house. I was sitting across the room and when Rich started loading a bowl I moved across the room to sit by him. When I took the first hit Tony's mouth dropped to the floor. I laughed so hard. He just couldn't believe I did it. I started smoking weed occasionally at first, and then it got to be an almost daily occurrence.

During that summer my foster sister told my parents that I was smoking cigarettes (not marijuana) and that I was dating Tony. They caught me in one of my biggest lies, and worst of all, when they confronted me about it I was drunk and stoned. I borrowed a relative's car so I could go see my friends and party with them. My parents were angry because they didn't think I should have borrowed the car. I don't think they knew that I was really stoned and drunk, although I was so scared of my parents being mad and catching me in a lie that my buzz went away pretty fast. We had a long talk and they told me that I wasn't allowed to ever talk to Tony again. They even thought of pressing statutory rape charges against him since he was eighteen. Somehow I talked them out of that. I was grounded for a month. I couldn't talk on the phone nor have my friends over. They even started looking at the mail I was receiving.

Since I was grounded I would baby-sit. I had my friends call and stop by there. I always found ways to get around things. I talked to Tony and told him that I was supposed to break up with him, but I wasn't going to. It was a long month, but my friends helped me through it.

The day I was "free," I was sent to my father's house in Minnesota for two weeks. It was just like being grounded again. I worked my ass off those two weeks. I helped around the house and did yard work. My father found out about my drinking and thought that if he got me really drunk that I wouldn't drink anymore. He was wrong. Now I have failed to mention that my father is an alcoholic and can have a bad temper. He got me so drunk I was sick and all he could do was yell at me. Since I was going home the next day he called my mother so he could talk to her. I had the hardest time trying to not let her find out I was drunk. Later that night my father and I got into a terrible argument. At one point he had me lying on the couch with my arms pinned down so I couldn't fight back. My little sister and next–door neighbor were there and they went to get my friend's dad so we could get my father away from me and calmed down. I was so happy when I left his house. I thought things would get better, but I was wrong. I still had a rocky relationship with my parents, and after my visit, my relationship with my father worsened.

When I returned to Iowa, I had an early curfew and it was still as if I was in trouble. I couldn't see a lot of my friends, but even still I was getting back into my old habits. Since things hadn't changed I decided to run away from home. I waited until a day when my whole family would be gone. I decided to leave on my aunt and uncle's wedding day. I told my parents I was ill, so I could stay home. After they left I packed my things and called some friends to pick me up. Later that evening the police were waiting for us when we returned. I was sent home with another aunt for the remainder of the night.

The next day we were supposed to leave on a family vacation, but my parents and I were not on each other's good side. I told them to go on vacation without me. I spent a week with my friend and her parents. When my parents returned we talked and things were better than what they were before. The next day school started. It was a summer I will never forget.

It didn't take long before I was partying all of the time again. Even though I had been in trouble all summer I still smoked weed and drank almost every day. The only thing I really learned was not to get caught again. Tony and I found ways to talk to each other. I was determined not to let my parents stop me from seeing him or my friends. If I went out drinking and I hadn't finished the bottle I was drinking from, I brought it home and finished it there.

I thought I was hiding things pretty good until I left my purse in my parent's vehicle one day. My mom looked in it and found letters from Tony. That night was the first night I told them that I loved Tony and wasn't going to break up with him. We came to an understanding that as much as they disagreed with it, I was going to be with Tony.

Tony got into trouble at the correctional facility and went back to jail. My parents let me out of school to see him in court. Watching my boyfriend being sent to prison was one of the hardest days of my life. I was allowed to give him a hug before they took him out of the courtroom. My last words to him were, "I love you." I cried for days after that. I felt like my life was over. That only drove me further into drug and alcohol abuse. If I wasn't at work or school, I was at a friend's house getting fucked up. I guess you could say that my friends were there for me, but not in the way they should have been. They did listen to me cry about Tony being gone, but there were also bowls to be smoked and alcohol to be consumed.

During this time I went to some wild parties. My friend Jeremiah drank all the time, so he threw a lot of parties. There were always drugs around. I remember being so drunk at one of his parties that I actually fell going up a hill to get to the keg. We had one party where everyone was standing in a circle just passing joints around.

I thank my friends for not letting me drive home every time I was drunk. I did drive home a lot, but was lucky enough not to get caught or in an accident. It took a long time for me to realize that driving home was really not a smart thing to do. At that time in my life I just didn't care anymore. Things in my life weren't going the way I hoped they would. My boyfriend was gone and I was really depressed. I wanted to spend more time with Tony.

I wrote letters every day telling him about what I did. Most of the letters I got in return were good. I could see he was hurting and that he did love me. Some of the letters were hurtful and angry, but I attributed that to him being in prison. I remember the day he proposed to me. It wasn't the proposal I had dreamed of, but it was a day that I had waited so long for. I wrote him right when I read it and told him that I would marry him. I was so happy, but it wasn't news I could share with my family.

Throughout this time I stayed friends with Mandy and became friends with her future husband. Mandy was one person that understood how I felt about Tony. We were very close. When Mandy's son was born he felt like my very own. When Dylan was a baby we were very attached. When he was fussy, no one could get him to quit crying except for me. I spent a considerable amount of time at Mandy and John's house. In my eyes it made sense to marry Tony since I was already part of the family. Tony and I decided to get married right after my eighteenth birthday.

After a while I started getting lonely. I wanted to see my fiancé. It's so hard, especially when you are young, to have a relationship with someone that you don't see. I was still getting drunk and stoned. I had acquired a wide variety of friends. I was meeting new guys. I wanted to be with someone I could go out with.

I met Joe and things changed. He had the same partying lifestyle as me. My relationship with Tony lasted for only a year. I still loved him, but I realized I needed more than he could give me. Joe and I attended all of the parties. I always knew where I could find a bag of weed or someone who was looking for some. One day I was hanging out in Hardee's parking lot with friends when some of my other friends pulled in and asked me if anyone was looking for a bag. Everyone in Newton knew I liked to party. My relationship with Joe was short–lived, but it was fun.

I met my friend Heather through Joe. She was his ex–girlfriend. We became best friends and spent every minute we could together. We worked at the same place and had a lot of the same friends. We did everything together. Heather was there for me when Mandy and I got into a fight because she thought I was sleeping around with different guys. She was wrong, and I didn't speak to her for over two years.

I did end up dating a "good" guy. Nick didn't smoke cigarettes or marijuana and he really didn't drink. He tried to get me to change. I didn't want to, so I hid my drug use from him. My friends still knew I smoked marijuana, but they didn't tell him. I guess one would say he got a rude awakening one day when I stopped into his workplace after smoking a fat joint with my friend Sarah. I stopped at the high school and picked Sarah up. While I was there I saw my friend Tim and conned him out of the joint. Sarah and I went to the river to smoke it and then I went to see Nick. He could tell right away that I was high. We got into a fight about it. My drug use affected our relationship because he didn't approve of it. Our relationship went downhill from there. We broke up a month later.

A couple of months later I met Jake. He lived in a larger neighboring city and had a house of his own. I was nineteen and graduated from high school at the end of the first semester. By that time I guess I had settled down. I didn't really drink that much and only smoked weed occasionally. Since I was out of school I was just working. Maybe that helped to slow me down.

Jake and I were perfect for each other. I fell in love with him right away. One month later we were living together. I told my parents I was moving in with my grandfather, but I spent every night over at Jake's house. Jake was perfect. He was almost too perfect. There was a side of him I didn't see for a while.

I knew Jake smoked weed all of the time, but that didn't bother me. Jake's temper started showing a couple of months into the relationship. It wasn't bad at first, but over time it escalated. I could see a little jealousy in the beginning. I had my friend's rehearsal dinner for her wedding the next day. Jake was angry because we went out for a while after the dinner. I wasn't doing anything wrong, but he still had me crying and feeling like this was my fault. I thought I was doing something right because I called him and told him where I was and what I was doing. Jake and I fought over the phone and also when I got home. I felt so terrible. I knew I shouldn't have gone out, but I thought it would be all right. Jake sent me a dozen roses at work. He apologized for the way that he behaved. That was all it took, and everything was forgotten.

Before I knew it, Jake was very controlling. He would get mad any time I talked to a guy. If I dressed up or wore makeup it was always for someone else. The only friends I could have were his friends. Things were bad, but I was in too deep to leave. I loved him so much. I kept thinking that things would get better, but I was wrong. I wanted to leave, but it took me six months to do it. I finally left when he started swearing at me when we were in the mall. By the time I left we were together over two years. I must say that all of this did not happen overnight. It took a while for things to get as bad as they did. If I had really thought about it, I never would have been with someone that verbally and emotionally abused me. I loved Jake a lot. He proposed to me on Thanksgiving in 1997. My parents were so happy because they liked Jake. No one really knew what he was like. I would just put on a mask and not let anyone know how things really were. When I say that Jake abused me I am happy to say that it wasn't physical. Jake never hit me, but I still feel to this day that had I stayed, the abuse would have turned physical and he would have seriously injured me. It was hard to leave, but I am a much stronger person because of it.

It took me a long time to get where I am today. Jake pushed my self–esteem down so low that it took a long time to get it back. I started partying again. I had my old friends back along with a lot more. I started going out to the bars and smoking weed again. When I was twenty–one I started dating Cory. That was when I really started to do things. I tried Ecstasy one night and I loved it. I took two pills my first time doing it. I was dancing and having so much fun. We rented a limo that night for a friend's birthday. I was drinking tequila and rolling. When we got back to our hotel room I was seeing people in our room that weren't really there. I was talking to them and when I reached out to touch them and they weren't there I wasn't scared. I loved to take Ecstasy after that. I was also trying coke. I didn't snort coke very often, but that was fun too. I was more open to a lot of things. My friends helped me find the side of myself I forgot was even there. I listened to different music and dressed differently. I wasn't the same person I was before.

To this day I still love to party as much as I did before. Even though I had some bad experiences, I wouldn't take back any of it. The guys I dated and the partying I did have made me the person I am today. I have high self–esteem now, and I like the person I am today. Someday I will settle down, but for now I am still partying and trying to live life to its fullest. I am now a college student and hoping to graduate in the next year. I am holding down two jobs. Life can be hard, but I have also learned that life is what you make of it. I made some aspects of my life harder on myself, but I have also made my life a lot of fun. Most of the stories I won't tell my children. Looking back, I ask myself how my parents ever put up with me, because I don't think I could handle it if my children were like me. I got caught in only a fraction of the things that I did. I wonder how my parents would have handled me if they knew about the drugs I did and all of the lies that I told. My parents are wonderful people. I had a stable home when I was growing up, but I think my desire to experiment gained control of me. Looking back I did some real stupid things, but I wouldn't trade it for the world.

(Names have been changed)

CRITICAL THINKING QUESTIONS

1. Why would a girl from a normal background become involved with someone like Tony?

2. Why did she become so involved in drug use?

3. With this background, would you be surprised if she were a good college student graduating with a major in criminology, and why?

9

From a Latino Gang Member to a Teacher in an Alternative School

Both of my parents migrated from Mexico and ended up in Texas. Most of my dad's side of the family is still in Mexico. I have five brothers, four of whom are older than me. My dad was a butcher and my mom was a seamstress, and as far back as I can remember, both my parents worked from sunup to sundown. We had a very close family and are still close. I had a normal childhood. I was never abused. I mean, I was punished, but I was never abused or neglected.

In sixth grade, I was involved in altercations in school, but I didn't start getting into trouble until I went to junior high school. I started hanging out with eighth graders, the wrong eighth graders. It started off with small things like fighting and pulling fire alarms. I was in and out of suspension, both in–school suspension and after–school suspension. It was at that time that I first got a taste of being in a gang. It wasn't like a major gang; it was just a group of friends who got together and decided to be called a gang. All we did was drink beer, smoke pot, and hang out at a house.

In my freshman year of high school, I started to get into more serious trouble. I got into a conflict with a guy for practically no reason. He just wanted to fight, but I didn't want to fight because he was older and bigger than I was. But even with the encouragement of friends, who were saying things like, "You can't let him punch you in front of your girl," "You're not going to do nothing?" and "I can't believe he did that to you," I still wasn't going to fight him until this guy who was part of the Crips came to me and said, "Take care of this guy. You know, we got your back." That's what he said: "We got your back." And I saw about ten guys standing with him, so I got pumped up and I said, "Alright let me go take care of this." Sure enough, I found him by his locker and we got into it. I threw maybe three or four punches before all the others jumped in and took his watch, shoes, and wallet. I got caught, but I didn't tell on anybody. I was approached by the same people again who said, "Hey, you didn't turn us in. You didn't get us in trouble. We want you to come join us." I didn't know exactly what they were involved in but I said, "Oh, fine, I'll do it."

Gang Activities

That's when I got rolled in. Let me tell you what it means to get rolled in. I remember it was after school. It was a pretty big deal because the head of the gang was there. Four of the guys were chosen from the gang for me to fight. I said, "Fine." I couldn't back out now because I'd already said, "Yeah." So they formed a circle around me, and we just went at it. I ended up fracturing one guy's hand. The big thing is that they couldn't knock me down. They were bigger than I was, but they couldn't knock me down. I gained a reputation from this as a guy who could take care of himself. From then on, I started doing what they wanted me to do and moved up really fast in the ranks. The second year that I was a freshman, I got into a fight with seven guys, and I got sent to a guidance center, which is an alternative center where they sent trouble makers.

That's when I started being involved more and more with the gang. I went from being a thug to being a soldier, to being a lieutenant, and nearly made it to be a captain. In a period of about four years, I went from being a regular kid to being a gang banger.

When I first started off, we were mainly involved in auto theft. I remember one night we went out and stole twelve cars. The easiest cars to take were Monte Carlos, GM Vehicles, Chevy trucks and Suburbans. We started by driving around town, taking the stereos, the tape decks, or CDs. We put them in our backpacks, dumped the car and left. We didn't have records, so we weren't too worried about fingerprints. We would go to open fields with the cars and just wreck them by playing bumper cars. They found five cars stored in one area, two cars found over here, another car found over there, and one found in the river. It was amazing that we were able to do it and not get into trouble. I still remember how to hot wire a car. If I had to, I could do it right now.

We also did a lot of drug stuff. My job early on was to take care of the block, which meant to keep an eye out. You made sure your territory is safe, and you made sure that no one is going to take your stuff. I also did a lot of peddling drugs, mainly marijuana. We would get about a pound or even two pounds and break that up into grams, which they called twenty dimes, half ounces, quarter ounces, or full ounces. By word of mouth, we would sell it to junior high school and high school students. A pound back then would cost about four or five hundred dollars; we could turn around and triple the money. The rest of us would split the $1500 between us.

We were sixteen and seventeen years old, with rolls of twenties in our pockets. We had nothing to with that money but spend it on junk. We would buy shoes and clothes. We took the girls out. We went to the mall like we were high rollers. Coming from the mainly Hispanic neighborhood we came from, the South Central side of San Antonio, your parents didn't have eight or nine hundred dollars to throw around like that. To see a kid our age with that much money, girls flocked to you. Guys wanted to be your friend. It gave you power, and you know that power corrupts. I was a seventeen–year–old kid with money in my pocket and a name that associated me with being tough.

I drove for drive–bys, but I never did any. Once you start getting involved in heavier crimes, you don't see too many drive–bys. You see more organized hits. I remember driving this guy to a house. He got out of the car, knocked on the door and asked for somebody. The guy came to the door. When he opened the door, he was shot on the spot. There was so much panic that he was able to get back into the car without even being recognized. I was scared, but I didn't show it.

It was at that time when the captain started realizing that I was more than a thug and more than a soldier. That was when he started saying, "It's time for you to do a little more for us. You deserve more power, more money in your pocket." I dropped out of school the next year when I was more involved in doing gang business. My parents didn't know.

I was involved in a shoot out one time. It was just like you see in a Bosnian or an Iraq war where you see people shooting at each other. A red Nova drove up to the house, and there was a guy sitting on a roof with a sawed off shotgun. I don't know what he was doing up there; you can't hit anything with a sawed off shotgun. All you can do spray pellets on people. He yelled, "Hey, the Ghetto Boys are in the neighborhood." The Ghetto Boys were the rival gang, and sure enough this gang got out of their car and started opening fire at the house. Little did they know there were five guys inside. The five inside the house went outside and opened fire.

I was out there standing in the middle of the yard. All you heard was pop, pop, pop, pop.

That's all I was hearing. And you could hear bullets whiz by your head. You feel the warmth of a bullet. I felt four or five go by me and hit the ground. I was not hit; some of the guys said that I was standing straight. Actually, I was standing there frightened, afraid to move because I was going to be hit. To them it looked like I was being a bad ass, just standing there just not caring about getting shot, just taking care of business, when, in fact, I was standing there frightened, frozen by my fears. So that gave me more status. They said, "Look at this guy standing there in the line of fire for us."

I never got caught. I was taken to juvenile hall one time, but it was for joy riding in a stolen car when I was seventeen years old. When you turn eighteen, your juvenile record is erased. So the following year, there was nothing on my record.

The reason I never got caught is because I was never at the wrong place at the wrong time. There was a house down my street that kept weapons, drugs and money. I was there almost on a daily basis, turning money in, picking guns up and dropping them off, dropping people off and picking them up. Whenever that place was raided, I was never there.

There are a couple of other things you should know about gangs. Gang recruitment is a big thing. When gangs recruited, they looked for people who were alone and who looked like they needed somebody. I know because I was involved in looking for those who were alienated by other kids and by the popular social groups. We also looked for the guy who was being picked on by jocks. In addition, we looked for the troublemaker, the guy who had in–school suspensions. We would say to them, "Hey, you know, we got your back." Or we would lie to them, "Hey, some guys said they're going to come after you after school. We won't let anything happen to you." They felt a sense of security and a sense of belonging as they started hanging out with us. They would get invited to the parties. Once you got them to commit, it is hard to get out, and so we say, "Hey, why don't you just become one of us? Let us initiate you."

Girls were property. We had a girl's gang that's affiliated with the guy's gang. The girl either got in by getting beat up by a group of girls or they got in by having sex with members of the boy's gang. You'd be surprised how many girls don't want to get beat up, and they'll take the roll of the dice. A group of guys would grab a set of dice and whatever number came up, that's what number of guys she had to sleep with. If it would be a hot girl, everyone wanted her and it would be more guys. If it was a girl that wasn't too attractive, it would be one or two guys.

The Disability

It was my disability that made me want out of the gang. You can't show any kind of weakness, and my disability was my weakness. My disability came from an accident that took place in December of 1996. I had just turned twenty–one. A friend of mine came back from being in Japan, and he wanted to go out. I decided, "Alright, we'll go out." My older brother, this friend, and I were driving back from the club, and we stopped to put gas in the car. While we were at the gas station, a car full of girls stopped next to us. We started taking with them. The girls wanted us to follow them to a party. We were so excited about the girls that we forget to get gas. Well, we ran out of gas. And we thought nothing of it because we knew there was a gas station ahead.

We got out and started pushing. I got behind the car with my brother. My friend was steering the car. Within a few minutes of pushing the car, we got struck from behind by a drunk driver. I was the only one that got hit. Another car came and hit me again. My legs got smashed. I remember lifting my leg up and seeing it dangling from skin and bones. I laid there in shock, bleeding to death until the ambulance came. I was awake through the whole thing, I never passed out. I remember everything. They scooped me up, put me in the ambulance and took to the hospital. Then, they put me on braces and had to resuscitate me twice with the defibrillator because I'd lost so much blood.

I was in the hospital from December to February, and I can't remember how many transfusions they gave me. The doctors finally came in and said, "Your right leg is completely destroyed because there's so much nerve damage. There isn't enough bone or tissue to reconstruct it. We can try to piece it together, but you'd have a high risk of infection. The only alternative is to cut it off." And so I ended up with a prosthetic leg.

Something that stuck with me at the time was when my mom told me one day, "You know who your friends are when you're in jail or in the hospital. If you go to jail or are in the hospital and nobody visits you, they are not your friends." When I was in the hospital, only one of my friends came to visit. Nobody in the gang ever came and visited me. That made me realize that the gang isn't family; it isn't true friendship. It's just a business; it's not that important. It was then that I finally realized that I needed to get out of the gang. I couldn't go on because those guys were either going to end up dead or in jail.

It took me a long time to get rehabilitated, and I hadn't had contact with any of the guys in the gang for a year and a half. Finally, I was able to contact them. I said, "Look! You can trust me. I can't do this no more, not with the condition I am in. I'm not going to rat you out."

The gang leader seemed to understand. He was an older man. He felt sorry for me because I showed up in a wheelchair, without a leg, and with all this hardware on the other leg. And he said, "Go ahead, drop your set, and if anything comes up, you know the rules."

The rules were very simple. If anything came down and was traced back to me, there went my life. Nothing ever happened! Nothing ever came back to me! I never ratted! I didn't have anything to rat. I also didn't have any heat on me. The leader knew that I did not know anything and that I didn't have any heat on me, so it was easier for him to say, "Fine. Get out."

I was able to leave the gang and try to go back to what I used to do. I worked for a summer doing manual labor and construction, but I couldn't do anything that had to do with physical activity because of my disability. I had to find a different avenue, so I decided to go back to school.

I have been in school ever since. I want to teach now, but I want to teach at the alternative school where I went and where they have all the knuckleheads. They have a high turnover of teachers there. Teachers teach for a year and quit the next year. They can't understand why students are the way they are, but I feel that I have been there. I know what it feels like. I have gotten out, but I want to be able to share. I want to let students know that it's not a done deal, that there are other ways out, and that they can turn their lives around.

CRITICAL THINKING QUESTIONS

1. Is it surprising that this person with a stable family background would become so active in gang activities?

2. What does this story teach you about gangs?

3. Are there any special features of Latino gangs that are apparent in this story?

4. Do you believe that this person will be able to connect with students in an alternative school? Why?

10

I Have Come a Long Way

I grew up in Chicago. I was the youngest of four children and I had both parents. My Mom was the authoritarian of the home. My dad worked a lot when I was very young, so he wasn't around a lot. He worked at night as a foreman of a factory, and every chance he had, he would try to better himself. This kept him busy, so my mother pretty well raised us kids. She was strict, but she did the job well. She took pride in being a mom.

Well, I always got in trouble in school. I was the class clown. I went to school about two blocks from my house, so I walked to school every day. I didn't put too much effort into being a good student. I never really thought of school as being very important, but I had to go because my mother would make me. I think I probably spent more time trying to get myself into trouble than I did working on my schoolwork. My teachers would call up my mother and tell her how much of a disruption I was during class, which led to me getting in trouble at home. But I wasn't always a disruption. I can remember that in fourth grade and sixth grade I was an excellent student.

I used to get into trouble by getting into fights all the time. I was bigger than the other kids. I guess I was a bully sometimes. If the person I fought with told my mom, she would then spank me. I used to vandalize cars with bricks. I was grounded for that, and my father had to pay for my damages. I was twelve or thirteen years old when I first got into trouble with the police. My friends and I would throw rocks at peoples' cars from above. The one rock I threw happened to land right on a police car's windshield. I ran from the scene. I went to a friend's house and cleaned up, and then I decided I was going to walk out and pretend nothing happened. As soon as we walked out, they grabbed us. The police put us in their car and told us to confess or we were going to go to prison. We stuck to our story and finally they took us all back to our homes. They told our parents that we were causing problems, but they didn't tell them about the windshield.

I remember when there were no gangs around my house, and then there was one guy who was a drug dealer who would sit at the end of our block. The guy would always come up to my group of friends and tell us to come and hang with him. He was planting a seed in our head to start selling drugs, and then we started to follow him around.

The next thing you know, we were a gang. Everybody in our neighborhood between the ages of thirteen through seventeen was part of a gang. The only reason I did it was because I thought it was cool that I could hang out with this cool dude, drinking beer and having people afraid of me. It was respect that we were all looking for.

One person started selling drugs, and he showed up one day with a gold chain. This caused a chain reaction, because others would then start selling drugs. Before you knew it, there wasn't a corner in my neighborhood where you couldn't get some crack. I was fourteen at this time. I started out as security at drug houses, where I would hold a gun and start shooting when anyone came over, like police, and such. I would tell myself, "Please don't let nobody come here." I did this hundreds of times.

Then I started to sell because I wanted to make some money. I remember one time when I was out selling. We saw these Vice Lords in our neighborhood trying to sell on our turf. I remember people were telling me to go and shoot at them. I remember the guy's exact words: "The nation do for you, now you got to do for the nation." Then the guy put a gun in my hand, and told me to get going. I started shaking as I walked down the street. I got up to the guy [the Vice Lord], and I had my gun in my hand the whole time I was walking toward them. About fifty feet away I raised the gun. When I got it up to eye level, they started to scatter and I just started pulling the trigger. Some guys dropped as they were ducking my bullets. This all happened so fast. I turned and started running. I wasn't sure if I shot anyone or not.

The whole time I was running I was thinking that this was stupid. When this happened, I was fifteen. After that happened, I went directly to school and came directly home. This situation made me think about things more. I decided to stay in school. I also started playing football so I would have a better chance of not going to jail. Football kept me busy.

I was blessed a lot of times. My life could have turned out a lot different. When I was in a drug house one time, I got this weird feeling so I left. I walked up the block and someone asked me what was going on down where I was at. I turned around and saw that the cops had raided the house where I was less than a few minutes ago. I got used to seeing some of my friends dropping out of school. Six of my friends ended up in prison and I went to five funerals when I was seventeen.

I went to college because my dad wanted it for me. My dad told me that if I go to school for one year and quit he wouldn't harass me about my future. But if I liked it, he said I needed to keep going. I started applying to colleges in March of the year that I was graduating high school.

I decided that I wanted to get away from Chicago, so I looked into this school in the South. This was a mistake. I went there for two years, and I saw more gang bangers and drug sellers than there were in Chicago. This was no different from home. All kinds of gangs were present on campus. But everybody from Chicago got along well even though we were in different gangs.

I got in trouble at college in December of 1993. I was in a dorm room smoking weed and the police came in. They took us all into the room and searched us. There was only one guy who had weed on him. The director of housing told the police to arrest us all, so we all went down to the county jail. They had us all processed into the county jail in 45 minutes. I had to call my father, so I could get money to get bailed out of jail. He wired the money to my roommate who bailed me out. This was a week before finals.

I was in a disciplinary trial at college. We got all kinds of charges. My father came down and talked to all the officials at the school. I was put on disciplinary probation. I went back to school the next semester and got into a fight with some other guys. One of the guys pulled a gun on my roommate, who called the police. The other guy got probation for pulling a gun and chasing my roommate around campus.

I decided to go to the college I am going to now. When my parents got a brochure, they sent it to me. I decided to come for a visit. On the car ride home from this visit, I told my parents that this is where I wanted to be.

I did not get into any more trouble my final three years of college. I was a better student than I had been before. Upon graduating, I got married last July. I am now working with juvenile delinquents in a residential center. My goal is to give back to them something that others had given to me. My life could have turned out quite different; I want to see what I can do for their lives to get turned around in a positive way.

CRITICAL THINKING QUESTIONS

1. Based on this story, how big of a factor is luck in whether some youths become delinquent or not?

2. How big of a factor were his parents in how his life turned out?

3. Have you ever had an experience in which your life could have been completely turned around?

4. Do you feel that this person would be effective in working with high–risk adolescents? Why?

Part II

BAD KIDS TURNED GOOD

It is always a glorious happening when a juvenile who has had all kinds of problems with the justice system is able to turn himself or herself around. With some of these writers, it took them longer to turn themselves around than others. With some of them, they had to go on to adult prison before they got themselves turned around.

11

I Was a Chosen Child

I was born at 11:41 PM on January 31, 1984. Both my mother and father worked at the hospital, which is where they met one another, so my birth was a big deal around the hospital. My parents were very well known around the hospital, and my grandmother and uncle also worked there during this time.

According to my parents, I was the most celebrated birth that the hospital had ever known. Hundreds of people came up to see me and visit with my parents. They told me that the nurses were astonished at how many people came to see me. Eventually they started telling the nurses that I was the governor's grandson as a joke to try and explain all the visitors that we were getting. I was one of the first mixed babies of an interracial couple to be born, and my parents were sort of famous for this I guess.

Early in my school days I was branded as one of the smart kids. Going into kindergarten I could already read and write and do arithmetic. The teachers talked to my parents about skipping me a grade, but they decided that it wasn't best for me. Thinking back on it now, I had somewhat of a discipline problem. I was always talking in class without "permission," which meant raising your hand, and I would occasionally be accused of "being off task." This is what the teachers used to say, but in all actuality, if it seemed like I was off task; it was because I was already done with whatever it was that they had assigned us to do.

I used to get very bored with the easy curriculum, and then I would get into doing other things that used to get me in trouble. It got even worse as I got older, because as things were getting harder and more challenging for the other kids, it seemed to get easier for me. I found myself done with all my assignments way before any of my classmates and I always got close to perfect scores. This had to upset some of my teachers.

When most kids are considered disciplinary problems, they rarely are at the top of the academic ladder as well. This makes it easier for the teacher to simply send them to the office or kick them out of class and dismiss them as if they'll never amount to anything, but I was different. I think it upset them more that I was one of their best students, and worst behaved all wrapped up in one.

Teachers and administrators were always calling home or telling me to have my parents come in and talk with them when they picked me up from school. It sounds really worse than it actually was though. If I had been just an average student, they probably wouldn't have cared so much; they would have just seen me as a bad kid who couldn't be controlled. But since I excelled in everything, I think they wanted to try and get to the root of the problem.

My parents had always told me when I was younger to keep my hands to myself. They'd say, "Son. I don't want to hear about you starting any fights. Treat people like you want to be treated. But if someone puts their hands on you, you have our permission to fight back and protect yourself" Those words always stayed in my mind and I tried my hardest to avoid confrontation at all costs, but eventually it became too much to deal with.

I don't know what it was about me, but it seemed like everybody wanted to "try" me. I was always one of the biggest and most athletic at everything, so maybe kids thought that if they could beat me up then people would like them more. Or maybe they thought it would boost their status in some other way. I truly don't know what their logical reasoning was for wanting to fight me, but someone always wanted to.

Being one of the biggest kids in school, who was always in a fight, probably made me look like a bully but I truly wasn't. I never picked on people or made fun of other kids, I was just different. People are always afraid of what's different. A big mixed kid like me didn't fit in anywhere. Yeah I was popular and had a lot of friends, but I never felt fully accepted in any group.

Fights on the playground and in school became something of expectation for me. I would get kicked out of school at least twice a year for fighting, but I didn't get in trouble for it when I got home because I was NEVER the one to throw the first punch. There were plenty of times where I should've been the one to throw first but I didn't. My parents' words were always ringing in my ears. "If someone puts their hands on you..." and that's always what I waited for.

I didn't lose any fights in my younger years and that makes things even more confusing to me. Why would kids want to fight someone who is notorious for kicking people's asses who messes with him? Maybe they thought they'd be the lucky one to put me down? I'll never understand those days of elementary school, but I can understand how my reputation preceded me into my next school.

My parents were very serious about my sister and I getting good grades. They weren't satisfied with anything less than our best. They pushed us hard and stressed the importance of education early on, and it came natural to us. I can't remember getting a B on anything until late into middle school.

There was about three or four months left until the end of the school year. We were all excited about being done with middle school and moving on to high school when this Hispanic, new kid from New York was introduced into one of my classes. Personally, I knew what it was like to be the new kid so I reached out to him. I was cool with him and we talked in class and in the halls and that was that.

Then one day out the blue, this little New York kid tells me he's going to be outside waiting for me after school, and he's going to kick my ass. I kind of shrugged it off like a joke because I knew that I hadn't done anything to him for him to want to fight me. Throughout the rest of that day a handful of people came up to me telling me that he had told them that he was gonna kick my ass. I didn't like how he was telling people what he was going to do to me so I was waiting for him outside after school but he never showed up. The very next day at school it seemed like everyone knew about the supposed beef between us. He was still running around telling people how he was going to beat my ass and all this other stuff, and people kept running up to me telling me all this stuff he was saying But I still hadn't seen this kid since the day before. Then after my third period class, I went down to my locker to get my other books. This was usually the part of the day when the Central Campus bus took us downtown but I didn't make the ride that day.

Standing by my locker I was confronted by this kid "I hear you been talking shit," he says as he walks up to me. "You the one talking about what you gonna do to me!" I fired back at him. By this time we started to gather a bit of a crowd. My locker was right in front of the office in the main hallway, so everyone in the passing period stopped to watch the drama finally unfold. A few more words were exchanged and then he swung on me. His punch barely grazed my cheek but it infuriated me. I tore into him with a flurry and, needless to say, we were going at it. Right there, we were going at it, in the hallway in front of the whole school.

We were scrapping for a good minute or two before any teachers tried to intervene. Even then, we were still trying to fight each other. I gave that boy the ass whipping of his life that day, but I don't even know why he wanted to fight me. When the whole thing was over and we were sitting in the office waiting for our parents to be contacted, I saw one of my teachers with an ice bag on her hand.

I asked our vice principal what happened to her and the vice principal said, "Don't worry about it. She'll be okay. It's not your fault." But I felt like it WAS my fault because it apparently had happened while trying to break up the fight. I didn't say anything more. I was too busy thinking about what my parents were going to say about me being suspended again for fighting. When my mom finally came to pick me up from school, they told me that I was suspended for three days and then I could come back.

Two days into my suspension we get a call from the school telling us that I'm suspended indefinitely and that charges are being pressed against me. This came as a complete shock to me. The teacher with the ice bag had unfortunately broken her pinky finger during the altercation, and she was pressing assault charges on me. The bizarre story that she told police went like this... She tried to break up the fight by pulling on my shirt from behind. Then, according to her statement, I stopped fighting this kid, turned on her and threw a punch towards her face and she blocked it with her hand and I broke her pinky with the punch and she had to get a ring cut off her finger because it swelled up so bad.

To this day this story makes me sick to think about. I used to get into a lot of fights with my sister when we were young, and my parents would always tell me never to hit women or put my hands on a female. That's just something that I would never have done. The only girl I've ever hit was my sister, and she deserved it when it happened. Other than that, I've never attempted to strike any woman.

Nonetheless, I'm kicked out of school; there's a story printed on the front page of the local newspaper spelling out my full name and saying that I assaulted some teacher and broke bones during the attack. I was going to have assault charges brought up against me, and to top it all off, the local system school tells me that I can no longer attend public schools in this district any where at all.

The school sent my work home for me to finish up the academic year, but I was prohibited from stepping anywhere on the property. My parents hired an attorney to represent me in juvenile court. I told this attorney my side of the story and gave him a list of over fifty people who had witnessed the fight. He went and got statements from all the people that he could get in contact with and they all stated about the same thing.

Every statement said that during the fight, the teacher, who I'll leave unnamed, was trying to pull me backwards by my shirt and lost grasp of it and slipped. They said that she had on high heels and lost her balance and fell back into the lockers. Not one of the witnesses ever said anything about me throwing a punch at her. I had no problem accepting partial responsibility for what had happened to her because of our fighting, since it wouldn't have happened if we weren't fighting. What I couldn't accept was being blamed for something that I honestly did not do.

This incident really screwed up my reputation. Even with all those kids' statements my attorney advised us that it would be easier to just plead guilty and get a deferred judgment. I did so unwillingly and was placed on a year's probation and forced to pay restitution for the ring that she had to have cut off her finger. To this day I think that's the only reason she pressed charges was to get her ring paid for. I would have been willing to split the costs with the other kid had that been an option, but instead the blame was placed all on me.

This is the summer where I became rebellious of everything. I started hanging out a lot more with the older guys in my neighborhood who were all in high school at the time. I can remember going home to get my curfew call from my probation officer every night, and then heading right back outside. Everybody that I knew had something to say about the incident at the school. It got so tiring trying to explain to everyone exactly what had really happened. The stress caused from being viewed as a delinquent who hits females was really taking a toll on me. I started to feel like I would never be able to get rid of the stigmatization. This is around the time when I started to drink heavily and smoke weed with my boys in the neighborhood.

I don't know what it was about the neighborhood that I grew up in, but it seemed like none of the gas stations or liquor stores really cared about whom they were selling to. If I had money, then nine times out of ten I could buy whatever I wanted. Occasionally, I would get ID by some attendant, but in that case we would just send someone else in to try their luck. If all else failed, we would just wait until somebody who looked cool came up and asked them to buy it for us. Either way we would always get what we had come for.

By the middle of the summer, a group of us were going through at least two to three fifths of hard liquor per day. We would be out drinking in the streets like it was nobody's business. Sometimes we would just sit in front of one of our houses all day and get really messed up in the summer's heat. Drinking hard liquor in the heat is not a good combination, especially for young adolescents with seemingly nothing else to do. It was a recipe for trouble that we knew very well.

It didn't take long for us to get bored sitting around drinking all night. We started walking the streets of nearby neighborhoods and breaking into cars to steal whatever might be of some value. The police were riding through our neighborhood regularly now. The older folks in the neighborhood, who were in their own criminal endeavors, used to try and talk to us and tell us to cool out on the shit we were doing. "Y'all making it hot around here!" they would say to us. They were right, but we didn't care. It was a like a game to us at that point. We felt above the law, and never thought we were doing anything seriously wrong. By the end of that summer, the Pizza Hut up the street from my house was closed down and a police station traffic unit was put in its place. Luckily for me, being on probation, I never got caught by the police for anything that summer.

With only about a month left to go in the summer, I got some good news from my attorney. He told me that I would now be able to attend the public school. I was so happy. It was too late for me to play baseball, but football season was right around the corner. The one condition was that I would also be on probation at school for the entire year. Any fighting of any kind would result in my expulsion from high school, and once again kicked out of the school district.

Going into my freshman year, the faculty and teachers already knew who I was. They knew about what had happened at my last school and it seemed like they all had it out for me. They were on my case about everything, and it felt like there were eyes o me at all times. It felt like I was walking on eggshells everywhere I went in the school. I would get written up and sent to the office for the most minor things. They must've been trying to test me and see what would make me snap so that they could kick me out and say, "We were right about you. It was just a matter of time." But I never gave them the satisfaction.

What I did though was stop caring about school altogether. My main homie would pick me up for school, and we would smoke a blunt on the way. At lunchtime it was the same thing, and after school it would continue on throughout the night.

After a while I started selling weed. It made it easier for me to smoke, and it put money in my pockets at the same time. I used to get some good shit dirt–cheap because I knew some big time people who would hook me up. I was making a killing at school. Well, it was probably only like $150 to $200 a day, but damn that's a lot for a fourteen-year-old kid with no job. I told myself that I would keep my stash on me at all times so that someone would have to search me physically to prove that I was doing anything.

Now, I bought a cell phone so people could get a hold of me and we could meet up somewhere. All afternoon and into to the evening we would just ride and smoke, and get money. The weed business gets kind of slow and old after awhile though. A lot of my partners were dealing crack cocaine and had been for sometime. They always tried to get me on that shit but it wasn't for me.

Dealing crack cocaine was like dealing death. I watched my boys pump that shit out hard and fast though with nothing on their minds but getting money. They never thought about the lives they were affecting, besides the ones they were dealing to. I've had family members hooked on dope and have seen first hand what it can do to a person and their family, and I wanted no part of it. Plus, I was no dummy. A little bit of weed on a juvenile is only a misdemeanor, but some crack is definitely going to get you a felony charge. These fools were out here getting hit with cases left and right and then going right back to doing the same shit when they got out.

One time, when I was out chilling on the block with my boys, the police came through and hit us up hard. There were maybe like ten of us standing out there and a handful of these guys had been working this spot for a while. Not me though, like I said, I didn't mess with that shit. Anyways, out the blue the police swarmed from all directions. They had squad cars, paddy wagons, and undercover units. There was no use in running. Anybody with any sense would know they weren't getting away from that. It all happened so quickly. Every angle was covered, but when you know you're facing some time, instincts will make you try to run even if you know it's no use.

The cops made their move. Guns drawn and ordering everyone to drop to their knees and put their hands on their heads, I followed their directions. A couple guys broke for it but they were quickly apprehended. I was clean so I figured I had nothing to worry about. They cuffed us and searched us all thoroughly. Luckily I didn't have much money on me that day or I probably would have gotten arrested too, but they let most of us go. People were driving by slow staring at us all in cuffs, just making it that much worse. This was my first time ever being in handcuffs, but it sure wasn't the last.

It was only by the grace of God that I didn't have anything on me that day. I was still on probation and any kind of charge would have screwed me. This encounter with the police really had me thinking about what I was involved with, and whom I was surrounding myself with. I made the decision to quit selling weed and narrowed my circle of friends.

School for me had turned into a place more for socializing rather than learning. My grades were terrible, and I didn't really care. Partying and getting wasted became my top priorities. I finished my freshman year with a GPA of like 1.5 or something like that. My parents felt like they had completely lost me and there was nothing they could do.

When that first summer of high school came around, we got real crazy. All the smoking and drinking began to make me paranoid. I stole my dad's .25 caliber semi–automatic pistol and took it with me everywhere that I went. One night after getting real high, my friend started suggesting that we go stick up this gas station to get some quick cash. Tommy was instantly ready to go. He grabbed his pistol and was up and ready to leave. His crazy ass kept his .22 Rifle loaded in his car at all times and he sprang into action.

But I said, "I ain't just gonna run up in there though! We gotta plan this shit out first." After only about an hour or so of planning, he and I were all in the car on the way to commit armed robbery. When we finally got to the gas station, it was closed. It was another blessing in disguise. Not satisfied with our botched plans, he drove to the other side of town where this party was going on. We drove past the house and saw people coming in and out of the party. He pulls around the corner and parks the car. "Y'all wanna get these guys instead?" We already had planned on doing the gas station so the stage was already set. I was to stay with the car and be in the driver's seat ready to go when he got back. I was cool with that. It had my adrenaline pumping real hard when we were going to hit the gas station but this didn't even have me nervous a bit. He got out the car with a mask covering his face and crept around the corner moving through the shadows.

I jumped in the front seat and turned the CD player back on low and just waited. A few moments later I hear a voice yelling over the music, "Stop! Freeze!" With the sound of the voice still lingering in the air I hear the report of the .22 being fired. Five shots in rapid succession, and my adrenaline was immediately pumping again. As I him rounding the corner in an all out sprint for the car, I threw it into drive before he even reached the doors.

"Lay down!" I said as he hopped in the car. I figured if I were the only one in the car visible, we would draw less attention seeing how there had been a gunman at the scene. I made it a point not to peel off either. I just eased off and drove casually back to Tommy's house. Once we got there we relaxed a little. He did not know who had come out the house yelling for him to "freeze." Tommy just started shooting and then fled. Luckily no one was injured and we never heard anything about it again.

About a week later Tommy came over to my house looking like he'd seen a ghost. He told me that he had gone with this other guy that we knew, and they had robbed this convenient store at gunpoint. They did it exactly how we had planned to do it. When they were done, Tommy got dropped off at this park and the other guy went to leave and got pulled over right outside the park's parking lot. Tommy sat in the park and watched his partner get arrested and taken to jail. He was so scared he didn't know what to do.

It was nearing the end of the summer and Tommy was getting ready to leave to go to college and play football, so he decided to just lay low. One afternoon, while hanging out in the neighborhood, the same guy who got arrested about two weeks earlier pulls up and hollers for Billy to come talk to him. Not thinking, Billy goes for a little ride with him. Not two minutes after he drops Billy off do the police swoop through and arrest him. I wasn't there but this is what he told me later on.

His supposed friend wore a wire and got him to talk about the robbery on tape. That's all the police needed to arrest him. This came as a huge shock to me to get the phone call from him down in county. I have to say that it shook me up pretty bad. At eighteen years old, he was sentenced to 148 years in prison. I felt bad for him but I also felt very lucky. I don't know why it took one of my closest friends getting locked up for me to realize what kind of dumb things we were doing, but it was a real wake up call. It gave me a real world look at just where my actions were going to lead me and I decided it was time to make a change.

I stopped drinking, slowed down a lot on smoking, and told myself there was no reason for me to be carrying around a pistol with me anymore. What I had my mind set on now was getting back into what I loved with a passion, football. By the time two–a–days started back up again, I was in shape and ready to play some ball. The coaches loved me. I did everything they told me to without question. By the end of camp, the coaches had me playing iron man football, starting on both sides of the ball, and I couldn't wait for the season to start.

In school now, I had a reason to apply myself to my studies again. I wanted to get my grades right and stay eligible to play football. It took a while for the teachers to notice that I had changed my ways, but they came around soon enough. By the end of my junior year, I was back on the honor roll and stayed out of trouble for the most part. I had a part time job and was living a clean life. Everything was going real smooth for me until about a month before my senior year of high school started.

We hopped in my Bronco, three of us only, and head to the liquor store. We bought a Texas fifth of Bacardi and pulled away from the drive–through. A block away from the liquor store we passed right in front of a police car stopped at a stop sign. The police car pulled out behind us and followed me up to the next stop sign. I signaled and came to a complete stop before initiating a right hand turn. When I turned, he put his lights on and pulled me over. My heart just about jumped up into my throat.

I was visibly shaken for a moment until I realized that we weren't doing anything wrong, except for being in possession of some alcohol. When the cop got out of his car, he walked up along the side of my car but didn't come all the way up to the window. In my side mirror, I saw him pull his gun out of his holster, and he told me to get out of the car. I was scared as hell not knowing what to expect now. His partner was on the other side of the car with his gun drawn, too.

They weren't pointing their guns at us, but it was still a threatening gesture. I slowly got out of the car and asked him what I was being stopped for. He didn't answer. Instead, he told me to spread my legs and put my hands on the back of the Bronco. I did, and he patted me down and told me to sit on the curb, which I also did. He then proceeded to take each of my other friends out of the car and do the same thing to them.

I asked him again what he had stopped me for and he replied, "I'm asking the questions here?" I didn't say anything else. The next question he asked was, "Do you have any drugs, guns, or grenades in the car?"

My homeboy snapped at this. "Does it look like we got some grenades in the car man? Be for real!!" he said to the cop.

Then, without asking for permission or having any probable cause, these two pigs hopped in my Bronco and starting searching it thoroughly. All they found was the bottle of Bacardi. They made me pour it out, and eventually told me why they had pulled me over in the first place. They said my license plate wasn't illuminated and gave me a ticket.

My senior year I was the captain of the high school football team, I won Homecoming King, and was an academic letter recipient. I felt like I was on top of the world. During the season I had a couple serious injuries that made me miss a few games but I still never missed a practice. My shoulder was separated on more than one occasion but I played through the pain. By the end of the season I was hurting pretty bad though. A bunch of Division II and III schools wanted me to come play football for them, but I didn't want to go to a junior college and play football. I wasn't even sure that I wanted to go to college at all.

The events of 9/11 made me realize that the country was going to war and I was afraid that they might enlist the draft again, so I made plans to try and get into college. Not long after, college football coaches were in contact with me. They came to the school to visit with my coaches and I, and they came to my home on a couple separate occasions. After taking an official visit up to one campus I decided that this is where I wanted to go to school. I was offered a scholarship to come here and play football, and I accepted the offer.

When I got up here for practice, things didn't work out though. My shoulder wasn't the same and I wasn't getting along with the coaches, so I decided that I was done with football. Even though I decided to quit football, I made the decision to stay and get a college education. I started out as a business major here but then I turned my focus more towards criminology. The reason I decided to switch majors is because I really couldn't see myself working in some cubicle all day when I'm done with school, and the criminology field was especially interesting to me because of all the things that I've been through in my short time here on earth.

CRITICAL THINKING QUESTIONS

1. What really went wrong in the life of this young man?
2. Whose fault is it? The school's? His peers'? His own behavior? His parents'? Or a combination of these?
3. Was being stopped by the two police officers an example of police harassment or of racial profiling?
4. He is ready to graduate from college now. Do you think he would work well with adolescents?
5. How do you see his future playing out in the life course?

12

Walking Away from Drugs Isn't Easy

My adolescent years were a real mess, but you would not have anticipated this because I come from a close and loving family. I have wonderful parents. My mother is an amazing woman. She was married to my father for twenty–five years and gave him six "miracles," as he called his children. Working at the YMCA for twenty years, she found her passion teaching swim lessons and water aerobics. She always managed to provide for us, love us, and be strong for us. Watching her husband dying must have been the hardest experience of her life, but she kept going for us. There were very few occasions when she ever fell apart. She was our rock and still is. My mother is now attending school to become a registered nurse

My father was a kind and thoughtful man, compassionate and true. He had achieved greatness in his life through his work as a social worker for twenty–five years, his parenting, and the lives of everyone he touched. He was the wisest and most compassionate man I have ever known. I think it is pretty special that to this day people still come to me and tell me how my father affected their lives. I still have not fully recovered from his death. One of my goals in life is to be the type of person my father was.

I recall endless days spending time with my large extended family and playing with my brothers and sisters. I remember church on Sundays and visiting the courthouse to see my dad working. I remember many positive affirmations and my parents telling me that I could do anything I wanted to do and be anyone I wanted to be.

My Siblings

In spite of all the positive influences in our childhood, three of the six children in our family really struggled in our adolescent years. I was the middle child in all my glory, but before I talk about me, let me say something about my other five siblings.

I will start with my older sister, the person that we all have so much admiration for. She was the caretaker and the pseudo–mother most of the time. The first day of kindergarten is a lovely experience for most kids but for me it was much different. I took seriously the affirmation of my parents that I could do anything I wanted to do and be anyone I wanted to be. After being told that I could not be a horse when I grew up, I barricaded myself on top of the bookshelf insisting I was indeed going to be that horse. After all, why would my parents tell me I could be anything I wanted if I could not? The nun who taught the class had attempted to smash my dream and that didn't sit too well in my eyes. In the end, my sister was called from her classroom to come and end my escapade. Seeing my sister come to the rescue was not an unusual happening in my childhood.

In her awkward teenage era, she dated an abusive boyfriend for three years. This started the pattern of abuse in her life that continued for seven years. Those men seemed to take the best from my sister. The spark in her eye is not there the way it used to be. They may have robbed her of her spark, but no one could take her dreams. She soared in college and today is attending an East Coast University pursuing a PhD. in criminology. She is happily married and has a beautiful baby girl.

My older brother, who was in and out of trouble all his adolescent years, has had a much different life than my older sister. My mother told me that they knew something was different about him at a very young age. He could be your best friend one moment and lock you up in a closet or fatten your lip the next. We were frequently rushed from the house because my brother was attempting to kill one or both of my parents. Life with him was completely unpredictable and at times very scary. Everything came to somewhat of a halt when my twelve–year–old brother was placed in a detention facility. He was institutionalized for the next six years, and this took a toll on him that could be seen in his eyes.

At the age of eighteen, he could no longer be held as a juvenile and was released. Upon release, he turned to selling drugs, a lifestyle that continued for four years. It was at that point that his world came to a screeching halt. A young man involved in a drug deal that went badly was beaten with baseball bats until he was nearly dead. Since this happened in my brother's house, he was sentenced to ten years for attempted murder even though he did not physically commit the act. After serving three years, he was released on strict parole. Since his prison term, he has been an absolute wonder. He is now studying to be a chiropractor and has not been trouble for anything since his incarceration.

My younger sister has also had her share of troubles. Growing up has been a tough experience for her, and she carries her battle wounds. Finding it extremely hard to adjust to life and to make friends, she turned to drugs and alcohol for her escape. Continuing on this road of self–destruction led to a suicide attempt that slapped us all in the face. Shortly thereafter, she was admitted to a drug rehabilitation center where she resided for five months. After what appears to be serious soul searching, she has found herself and sobriety, and has stayed clean for the past year.

I also have two younger brothers who have not had any problems in childhood. One is very intelligent and now, at eighteen, is very much into politics and history. He is looking forward to going to college. The youngest child in the family is a long–haired skater boy who is into singing and drama. He is now fifteen and instead of pursuing adolescent trouble, he has turned inside to positive interests and activities.

My Deviant Activities

As for me, I attended a Catholic grade school. This meant no nonsense, church on Fridays, nuns for teachers, and occasional spankings and pinches for misbehavior. On the plus side, we had better food than the public schools. We wore uniforms made up of navy pants and white button–up shirts. My siblings and I were able to attend this school through scholarships the church gave out to families in need, but we never knew we were any different.

I found myself in trouble quite often. In music class, my permanent place became a bench in the front of the classroom right beside the nun. In the fourth grade, another boy and I had a running bet on who could be sent to the principal the most in one week.

The summer of my sixth grade year brought my first experience with alcohol and marijuana. When it came to that first drinking episode, the last thing I remember was falling down a flight of stairs and cracking my head open on a wall. I also remember the smell of dried vomit and the vow to never drink again. If only I had kept that frame of mind, my childhood would have gone quite differently.

The marijuana use came shortly thereafter. My older sister would bring me over to her boyfriend's house to hang out, and the lovely people over there thought it would be funny to see how stoned they could get the little one. It turns out smoking pot was something I enjoyed, so it became an activity in which I would frequently partake. The only small problem was keeping it from my family.

At this point the turmoil, in my family was mounting. My brother was in an institution, my sister had moved to live with relatives, and we just discovered my father had terminal cancer. The day we sat down around the old wooden table to hear about our father was a devastating blow. Multiple myloma is what they called it. To my thirteen–year–old ears, they were foreign words. My youngest brother was just six years old. Our new reality was trip after trip to the hospital in Minneapolis and weeks at a time in hotel rooms while Dad endured chemotherapy. Eventually, we did return to some normalcy. Our lives were different from that point on, but we had to go back to a routine for fear of falling apart. .

Not knowing what direction to take, I made bad decisions in my life. I turned myself inward and increased my drug use. Methamphetamine was my new drug of choice, and I used it almost every day. While my family was with my father having his bone marrow transplant, I was getting high. I missed out on all the time they spent together learning about each other. This is something I will regret forever. Things did go well for my dad, and he was in remission for three years.

For myself, I continued my marriage with drugs. Meth, pop, acid, cocaine, mushrooms, GHB, alcohol, and anything else I could get my hands on. I was using meth and coke intravenously at the age of fifteen when I decided that running away to Nevada was the true path to happiness. So, two of my friends and I packed up and left the state. We were pulled over in Elko, Nevada, and arrested as runaways.

Upon arrival at the detention center, I was strip–searched and found to be in possession of methamphetamine. I was eventually charged with being in possession of meth, marijuana, alcohol, and being a runaway. My parents were contacted, and they were told to come and get me. They did that, and it was the longest drive of my life. My father was so angry I think he yelled and cried half the way home. I was such a rotten child to him. I had somehow managed to make him feel that all of my problems were his fault.

Upon returning home, I was sent to a juvenile detention facility until a bed in a drug treatment facility opened for me. Two weeks later, I was spending my days at this drug treatment center. I managed to make my thirty days there and was sent to a halfway house that specialized in adolescents with drug addictions. Family therapy sessions helped guide me to the realization that I was hurting not only myself but everyone who cared about me. I look back now and cannot imagine how my parents were so strong through everything I put them through. They never gave up on me.

Although I had every intention of cleaning up my life, I was just not able to do it. I ran away two times and continued my drug use. On one occasion, we stole a rusted out station wagon and drove to the southern part of the state. After a long drug binge, I was caught. Somehow, I convinced my probation officer that sending me home was the answer to my problems. I told him that I was going to do good if I could just go home.

Well, that lasted about three weeks. I was caught in a drug house with needle in hand. After an altercation with the arresting officers, I was sent to a detention center for holding. That was a miserable time in my life. I didn't speak a word for two weeks, except to my parents on the phone. There was no pleading out of this one as I had more charges pending. With the threat of training school weighing on my shoulders, I began to work the program.

My probation officer pulled some strings and managed to get me into this drug treatment center with the threat of the training school if I messed this one up. This treatment center was the first time I really took my recovery to heart. I wanted to be sober and to live without drugs. I wanted a relationship with my family, and most of all, I just wanted to be home living a normal life. I worked hard and, with the support of my family, was able to successfully bridge the program in six months. Finally, I had found some peace and contentment in the person who I had become. I was proud and ready to face the world.

Things were good for a long time. Attending intensive aftercare and Narcotics Anonymous meetings kept me in check with sobriety and refraining from drug use. I excelled academically while attending an alternative high school and was able to graduate one year earlier than anticipated. All I had to do was keep the monkey off my back, so to speak. The responsibility I carried at home was also helping me to stay clean – being that my brother was in prison and my sister was in college. I was the oldest sibling at home, and the one that my mother needed the most help from. My father's cancer had returned, so he was in Minneapolis receiving treatment. At home, I was in charge of getting the kids to and from school and other activities.

Dad came home on a Sunday night after a long hospital stay. We could not have been happier. I prepared a meal, and we had a cake for the homecoming. The bliss did not last long though. My mother woke me at about 5:00 the next morning and told me to go wait outside for the ambulance because my father was having a seizure. Shortly thereafter, the ambulance arrived and took my catatonic father to the hospital. After weeks of sleepless nights and endless days, our prayers were answered. He recovered; we saw it as a miracle.

We went home to return to normalcy again. After a year of sobriety, I relapsed. My new boyfriend and I had started on a path to destruction, using once again. It did not take long to get in over my head. We were selling drugs out of our apartment and using meth almost everyday. We had gotten into manufacturing the drug at the farmhouse of our friend. Never thinking that what I was doing could send me to prison for a long time, I continued to play a major role in this process.

I hated manufacturing meth though! Every breath was torture, the burns hurt your skin, and the process was complicated and lengthy. Still, it continued until an overdose left me shaken to the core.

It was a rainy Saturday afternoon when I decided to get loaded with my so–called friends. Fixing myself up a hit, I ignored the warnings that this batch was different, that I should not take so much. As the drug found its way into my system, I knew instantly I should have been more careful. Before I blacked out, I remember shaking and babbling incoherently, trying to get across that I was going to be okay. I awoke in a bathtub with all my clothes on and feeling like complete dirt. At that moment I made the decision that my life was going to change. No longer was I going to be a slave to drugs! My life was going to be different!

Recovery

Coming clean to my family was the first step I had to take. It was a devastating blow to them to hear that I had gone back to drugs, but they continued to stand by me. My dad meanwhile had taken a turn for the worse. A hospital bed was placed in our living room; wheelchairs and hospice nurses were always around.

After Dad was moved to the hospital, things went rather quickly. Knowing that he would soon die brought on feelings of guilt, anger, and sadness I did not know I possessed. I spent hours by his bedside talking, telling him how sorry I was, laughing with him, and discussing my future.

June 30, 2000, is the night my father's soul left this earth—a night forever etched into my memory as the worst night of my life. We all sat around his bed holding hands and singing to him as he left this earth. Not wanting it to be true, I climbed into the bed with him, holding him just one more time. How do you begin to say goodbye to the most honorable and true man you have ever met?

I made the decision that I would try to hold the type of candle that my father had left in this world. I graduated from high school and went on to community college. I had a major challenge when I became pregnant. Being only nineteen, I was devastated and scared. My daughter's father could not decide if he wanted to be a father or not, and he was in and out of the picture.

I graduated from community college and went on to a four-year college. Once I was in this school, I declared a major in criminology, hoping to work with troubled youth, and managed to get good grades. Soon after, my father's daughter joined us. He has grown into a wonderful man, father, and person. Being from a family like mine has taught me how to be a good mother, girlfriend, and person.

As I come to the end of my college career, I am pregnant again. There are also decisions to make: whether or not to continue past my bachelor's degree, when to get married, and where to live. I try to remember that the paved path is not always the best one to take. My father told me to try to take the unpaved road and to stand tall in my challenges. Decisions will come and go, but family is constant. I make every effort to make my daughter's experiences memorable and comforting.

Writing this paper has brought tears and laughter, warm and hurtful memories. It is important to look back and remember where we came from, where our roots are, and why we are the people we are. Remembering my father and the impression he has left on my life has been especially meaningful for me. Taking the unpaved road, standing tall in the face of adversity, and honoring his memory in all of my being has brought me to where I am now.

CRITICAL THINKING QUESTIONS

1. How do you think it is possible to struggle so much in childhood when you have a loving and supportive family life?

2. Why was it so hard for the writer of this story to walk away from drugs?

3. How would this story be different or have a different outcome if she and her friends had been arrested and convicted of manufacturing meth?

4. The writer of this story sees her father as a person who touched many people during his life. What characteristics does one need in order to be a positive influence on others?

13

Wrong Place at the Wrong Time

My life started out as a breeze, but only because I wasn't aware of the things that were going on around me. Up until the age of eight, my mother, father, brother, and I all lived together right outside of town. I lived in an environment that looked normal but was the exact opposite. I lived in a home of alcohol abuse, physical abuse, and drug abuse. There were many nights that my brother and I had to stay with family and friends because my father was drunk and hitting my mom. My mom handled herself the best she could. She would leave for the night if she knew he was just looking for a fight. There were numerous nights when my father was escorted away by the cops. I also encountered many drugs as a child. My parents did drugs, and there were nights when we watched them shoot up. There was also a lot of drug abuse at my aunts' and uncles' houses.

My brother and I were sent on these dreaded trips to California during the summers to see our father's parents. My father was a truck driver, and he would leave us there for weeks while he made a trip back to his home base and then back again to California to pick us up. I hardly ever enjoyed the time that I had to spend with my grandparents. They never treated me as if I was their grandchild. My brother was very spoiled by them. I, on the other hand, wasn't. They took him shopping many times for new clothes and toys. I would get maybe an outfit or a toy. I think they thought that I was too young to notice that they were doing this, but I still remember it to this day.

One story that sticks out in my mind happened the summer that my parents separated. I wanted a Cabbage Patch Doll, and my grandmother refused to let me buy it. Her excuse was that there wasn't enough room on the plane. Although it was my money that I had been given to spend while I was in California, I wasn't able to spend it on what I wanted. Instead, she had me buy some Barbie clothes. I didn't even play with Barbies. My brother got to buy a live lizard that summer. Kind of odd how I couldn't buy a Cabbage Patch Doll, but he could get a live lizard. I still recall the comments that they used to make around me and not think that I understood. I remember them calling me "the mistake" or the "unplanned." It was also the attitude they always seemed to have that made me feel as if I was a mistake.

This same summer of the Cabbage Patch Doll incident, my mother decided that she'd had enough of the abuse in the house. So she left my father. She packed everything up and moved us into a house in town. When my father returned from dropping us off in California, he came home to an empty house. The bedroom furniture was all that was left. There wasn't a dish or a towel in the house for him to use. That summer was one of the turning points in my mom's life, as well as in my life and my brother's.

My brother and I weren't aware of what was going at home, but we were soon to find out. Our family seemed to think that we shouldn't hear about this while we were in California. That summer, rather than riding in the semi-truck with my father, we flew back from California. I have to say that it was my first and probably my last time in a plane. When we reached home, my grandparents kept my brother and me at their lake home, about twenty-five minutes away from our house. They kept us there for three weeks – two weeks longer than we were supposed to be with them – so that my mother and father could have some time to talk about things.

What my father and my grandparents didn't understand, though, was that my mother was done. She had truly had enough. She had put up with abuse and fighting for eleven years and things hadn't gotten any better so she needed to just get away. I knew I didn't want to see my parents get a divorce, but I also knew that my mom wasn't happy.

I remember seeing her cry many nights when my father and she had gotten into it. I remember seeing her with bruises on her arms, legs, and face. I remember one night when my father was out drinking with his buddies. He decided to come home and fight with my mother. When she opened the door, he grabbed her and threw her up against the wall by the door. He threw her to the ground. Josh and I were lying on the couch watching a movie when he came over to us. My father yelled at us to go to bed, so Josh and I went to our rooms. We could hear my mom screaming and yelling. Josh ran out of his room and into the dining room to call my grandma, who called the cops on my father. It felt like it took the cops forever to get to our house, but it was only seconds until everything was over. After that, I was scared to visit my father. I didn't know if he would hit us like that if he got mad at us. Josh didn't seem to even care what was going on with our mom. He was seeing it as: that was his dad and he was going to be around him no matter what.

Peers and Trouble

The next few years of my life were spent commuting back and forth to school. We got up with my mother every morning, and she would take us to our father's house on her way to work, where we would then get on the bus and go to school. My father was still living in the house in which my mother had left him. When my brother turned fifteen, he started driving us back and forth to school since he had a school permit. This didn't last long because my brother got into the wrong crowd and started skipping school. This left me with finding a ride to school or riding the bus. Well, my friends and I got into the same routine as my brother and his friends with not going to school. This is where the next turning point in my life was.

The friends that I was hanging out with at this time didn't have curfews, rules, or parents who cared if they were going to school or not. We used to hang out until all hours of the night doing things that I now can't believe I was doing then. We were drinking with people who were anywhere from five to eight years older than us. Obviously, we had them buying alcohol for us. If we didn't have anyone else to do it, we would stand outside of a bar or gas station waiting for someone so we could ask them to buy for us. Usually, we came across some type of buyer for the alcohol. If not, we also had friends who would go to the store and steal it for a cheap price. Drinking seemed to always lead us to more trouble than we needed to get into. There weren't really any hangouts or places for teenagers to go, so we decided to drink and find our own entertainment. We would either vandalize some place, like taking light bulbs and breaking them on the street, or we would start fights with other people.

My thirteenth birthday is one birthday that I will never forget. One of my friends and I were staying at my father's house for the weekend. My father was out of town on one of his trips. We were supposed to be supervised by his roommate, but at the last minute he decided that he wasn't going to be around. We decided to stay anyway and not say anything. This is when everything went wrong.

We wanted to go to town and pick up some friends to hang out with us. We couldn't find anyone to come get us, so we decided to borrow my father's car and go get them. Neither of us was old enough to have a license, so by driving we were already breaking the law. Well, my girlfriend decided she could drive. We picked up a couple of our friends, but we didn't want to go back right away so we decided to go to the mall and hang out. We ran into some more friends of ours at the mall who wanted to get a ride home. We gave them one and this is when everything went all wrong. For some odd reason, when we pulled into the driveway of the house where we were dropping our friends off, the girl who I was with pulled all the way into the garage. When she went to pull back out, she turned the wheel and caught the center divider of the garage and pulled the front of the garage down. The whole thing didn't fall down, just the front part. It was bad enough though. Well, she panicked and left the scene. When this kid's parents got home, they called the police and told them about the whole situation.

The police were then looking for us. For the rest of the day we cruised between all the small towns in the area not knowing that the police were looking for us. Our parents and families had all been contacted and they were looking for us too. We finally went to my father's house around 10 p.m. that night, and this is where my oldest cousin, Tony, found us. He was so mad at us. He told us to get in the truck with him and that he was taking us to his parent's house before the police found us. When we were driving down the highway towards his parent's house, about six police cars went by. I watched them as they turned into my father's circle driveway. When we got to my aunt and uncle's house, they let the police know that they had found us.

That night I met this police officer. He came into my aunt and uncle's place like he was a drill sergeant. He spent the next hour or so yelling at us and trying to scare us as much as possible. He told us that he was going to be our worst nightmare. He said that any time that we messed up until the day we died he was going to be there to remind us of this very conversation. I wasn't even scared of him. The only moment that I remember being scared was when he took my friend away and put her in the police car. He had to take her away because her father was too drunk to pick her up and had filed a missing persons report on her. Therefore, they had to take her into custody. I was tripping out that my girl was getting hauled into jail.

The Juvenile Justice System

From the ages of thirteen to fifteen years old, I was pulled over by the police on several occasions. It seemed like I was always getting hauled to the police station. I was put on probation for a year at the age of thirteen for a car theft. Within a few months of getting off probation, I dropped out of school and found myself getting into more trouble.

Not very long after I dropped out of school I was put back on probation for a vandalism charge. There were six of us involved, and I wasn't the only one who received this charge. The charge came from stealing light bulbs out of a local hotel bathroom and smashing them on the sidewalk of the main street. While on probation for this charge, I was busted again and was sent to a girls' home for a thirty–day evaluation. After returning to my mother's house at the end of these thirty days, I went right back to hanging out with the crowd that I was supposed to ignore. Things didn't change for us. We were still out getting into trouble and finding it wherever it may be.

Less than six months after I got out the first one, I was sent to another facility for another thirty days. This still didn't get me to straighten up. Within six months of being released from that facility, I was back sitting in front of my probation officer. He said he was fed up with seeing me and having to deal with me. He wanted to find something that would scare me straight. He did just that. That very next weekend, he and I took a long road trip to Leavenworth, Kansas.

He took me to a girl's boot camp for juveniles who had been in trouble or who just needed to be scared straight. The road trip in the car was bad enough. There were long moments of silence when he would ask me questions like why did I do the things that I did and why did I choose to follow a path in my life that wasn't going to get me any further than jail or the morgue. To me, I just figured this was his way of trying to scare me, but now that I think about it, I think he was really trying to get an understanding of me.

The boot camp really did a job on me. I was scared to death of having to live in a facility like that. I didn't want to be that far away from my friends or my family. I also didn't want to deal with the things that the girls there had to do. There was far too much discipline and hard work at the camp for me. My probation officer had done his job and scared the crap out of me.

The Accident and Its Consequences

A year passed before I had any type of run–in with the police, and this time I didn't get tied up in criminal charges. I was involved in a drunk driving accident. It was July 24, 1995, when a few of my girls and I decided to go to a bar at a lake resort town. This was located about twenty minutes from our hometown. We had been drinking most of the day before we finally found a ride there. We hung out in the bar until it closed. After the bar, we went to our usual hangout, which was a lot across the street from the only gas station that was open.

We looked everywhere for a buyer to get us alcohol. We found one and he stocked us up with three eighteen–packs of beer. There were three carloads of people going and at least five or six people in each car. While drinking out at the lake, we were telling creepy scary stories and freaked some people out. We hung out for a little while longer and then headed out to drop people off. It was already after three o'clock in the morning so we knew that we needed to start taking people home. We didn't make it far.

We got the first person home and while coming out of her driveway, we went off a T–intersection. We had six people in the back and three of us in the front. I was sitting in the front seat on somebody's lap and did not have my seat belted on. I flew out of the windshield and landed at least thirty yards in front of the car. When the paramedics got to the scene, no one had seen me or been able to find me. Somehow I crawled out of the ditch and my friend found me. I wasn't breathing very well, and I wasn't looking very good either. She helped me breathe by telling me to breathe in and out. She told me later that I was trying to lie down and go to sleep. She yelled for the paramedics to help her and that was when I totally blacked out. I was flown right from the scene of the accident in a helicopter to University Hospital.

Upon arriving at the hospital, I had already flat lined two times in the helicopter, each time for more than four and a half minutes. My head injuries were life threatening, and the doctors gave me less than a 30 percent chance of living. I broke three different vertebrates in my back and neck. I had crushed all the bones in the right side of my face and needed reconstructive surgery for that whole side of my face. I also broke the hard pallet in the top of my mouth and my jaw in three places. My mouth was wired shut for six weeks. I went through over fourteen hours of surgery to reconstruct my face and wire my mouth shut.

I broke my clavicle bone, two ribs, and my right wrist. Most of my teeth had become loose, and I had lost the top front two, so the doctors had to reset all of my teeth before wiring my jaw shut. I spent four days in a sedated coma and three more days in the hospital. I couldn't stand up alone or even get in and out the bed by myself. I had to have help with everything that I did. At the age of fifteen, I had to depend on my own mother to wipe for me and help me bathe.

I took this accident and used it to my advantage rather than letting it hold me back. Before the accident, I had been running with a crowd of people who weren't going to school and who were always looking to get drunk and find trouble. Well, I'd had enough of this life style. I wanted to make a change. While going through all of my rehabilitation from the accident, I got back into school. I was enrolled in an alterative school that was located forty–five minutes from home. Not having a license made it difficult for me to get back and forth. I had a few friends who attended the same school, but they weren't ones who went to school on a regular basis.

By the end of my junior year, I had twenty–five hours to make up if I wanted to graduate on time. I was living at my brother's house with him and his girlfriend and it wasn't working out. I needed to find a house where I would be able to stay and also be able to make it back and forth to school. My senior year, I moved in to my grandmother's house and had my grandpa take me to and from school.

When I was in the eighth grade, I promised my mother that I would graduate on time because my brother had dropped out. I was going to keep my promise. In my senior year of high school, I made up all of my credit hours from my sophomore year, my junior year, and my senior year. I graduated on time with my class and with honors. I had the highest grade point average (CPA) that I had ever had, and I was more proud of this than getting my actual diploma. I knew that my GPA showed exactly how much time and work I had put into school. I had gone everyday from 8:00 a.m. until 4:00 p.m., and some days I had stayed longer or gone earlier. To see the smile on my mother's face when I walked up the aisle to accept my diploma was the best thing that I could have seen at that moment. It reminded me of all that I had put her through.

College Years

Soon after graduation, I moved into an apartment on my own so that I could attend a local community college. I thought that everything had turned around for me until I moved into that first apartment. I had a roommate who ran with some bad friends. One of them decided to sell methamphetamines out of my house. Well, he obviously did it many different times without me knowing. He did it enough times to have the apartment investigated by the police. A confidential informant entered my house on December 17, 1997, and purchased some methamphetamines from a friend of the original guy. I wasn't around at this time because I was out running errands.

A few months later my roommate and her boyfriend got picked up for marijuana, and they were questioned and accused of the incident in December. They soon had my roommate and me in custody for the December incident, questioning us about what happened on that specific day. Our word really didn't mean much in the whole investigation. They accused us both of being guilty by association. We were both charged with more felonies than I can recall. I was charged only because my name was on the lease and they wouldn't believe that I didn't know that methamphetamines were being sold out of my house. We were supposed to go to trial but we made a plea bargain.

This was the last straw. I was tired of dealing with the system and I surely didn't want to live in it for the rest of my life. I was sentenced to thirty days in jail and had to pay a $750 fine. I was also ordered not to get into any other trouble or the original charges could be brought back up, which would mean at least fifteen to twenty–five years in jail and least four felonies on my record. I was attending college at this time so my jail time was put off for a few months.

During this whole investigation, I was seeing a man, who was apparently wrong for me. Because of the investigation on the apartment, I moved to another apartment and he moved in with me along with another one of his friends. During the first few months, he was more than I could ever ask for or expect but the bad side soon came out.

My boyfriend was very jealous of my friendship with our other roommate. One night he had the audacity to hit me. He struck me more than once. At first I didn't respond to it. I left and stayed at a friend's house for the night. But that wasn't the only time that he hit me. Don't get me wrong! After that first time, I swore that I would never let him do it again without out me hitting him back. The ending point of our relationship was set off with our last physical altercation. He had grabbed me around the neck and tossed me across the room. Our roommate heard this going on, and when he came in to see what was going on, he found my boyfriend hitting me across the face with his fist.

My roommate grabbed him to stop him and hold him back so that I could get away. I did just that but only after I hit him a few times. I wanted him to know what it felt like to be hit by someone whom you care for and whom you trust, I ran out of the house and had gotten in my car to leave when he opened the car door. I didn't stop, though. I backed up, which caused him to fall. I drove straight to my mother's house to get help. I stayed there for the night and for the next few days. We finally talked and said that things needed to change otherwise one of us was going to end up dead.

Not long after this conversation, I turned myself in to do my thirty days in jail. I checked in to jail on January 4, 2000. I spent the next month in jail doing time for a crime that I didn't commit. I had lost my boyfriend and wasn't real sure of where I wanted to go with my life from there.

A month before, my uncle had been sentenced to five years at a federal penitentiary. With both of us being locked up, times were hard for my family. My grandmother wasn't in the best of health as it was. The month that I did in there was the longest month of my life. It was a lot of thinking time and a lot of time to put my priorities in line. Two weeks after my release date from jail, I lost my grandmother.

I realized that day that I only had one life to live. I had to change everything about my life if I wanted to get past the drama I had been involved in and make something of myself. I stayed in school to finish my two–year degree and worked three jobs in the process.

Now it is three years down the road. I have earned a bachelor's degree in social work and now I am working on my second bachelor's degree in Criminology. I am planning on getting my master's degree and someday getting my doctorate.

I know that I haven't had the best of luck, yet I have managed not to let things hold me back. I am on a mission in my life to accomplish getting my degrees and to have a good life. So far in my life, I have chosen to go down the wrong path on quite a few occasions, but by being stubborn, curious, and driven, I have gotten through it all. I don't look back and regret any day in my life. I am thankful for each and every experience that I have been through. I have watched and seen many things in my life that I know many people will never have the chance to see or to experience.

CRITICAL THINKING QUESTIONS

1. What negative influences did this young person have that contributed to her delinquent behaviors?

2. Did she become better or worse from the time that she was under the jurisdiction of the justice system?

3. What choices did this person make that led her down the wrong path?

4. Why did this person permit herself to become involved in the abusive behaviors that her mother had experienced and that she had observed in the home?

5. How would you feel about being taught juvenile delinquency by this person once she has learned the necessary academic credentials?

14

I Want What Other Kids Want

I was born at Mercy Hospital, which is located on the South Side of Chicago. At the time of my birth, my mother was sixteen years old and my father was 21 years of age. My mom was the first to have a child out of three sisters and five brothers, which makes me the oldest out of all my cousins on my mother's side of the family. One of the things that I can remember about my childhood is that I received a lot of attention from my family, despite the fact that I have 23 cousins that were born after me. In most families, it is usually the last born that receives the most attention; however, that is not the case with me.

The Walk

When I think back to my childhood days, I have few memories about my father. The reason for this is that my dad was not around very much. One of the things that I remember the most is the day I went to see him in prison. I think I was about ten years old. This is one memory that sticks to me like Krazy Glue and is something I will never forget. Walking up to those prison walls with my grandmother holding my hand was one of the scariest things I had to do. No nightmare or any ghost story could have compared with that walk I had to make. It was not so much how the prison looked that terrified me, nor was it the way the guards stared and searched me that made me shake, but the thoughts I had about people being caged like dogs. My father stayed there for six years for killing a man. That was my first visit to a prison, but not my last.

Seeing my dad in that situation made me look at things in a different way. For example, going to the zoo with my school or with my mom and cousins was something I had always loved to do. After seeing my dad in prison and watching him leave the visiting room in a slow–like motion made the zoo a not–so–fun place anymore. It killed me to look at the animals in their cages. I felt sorry for them all.

Dear Old Dad

My mother did not talk much about my dad at all, and when she did, it was not in a positive way. I can remember her saying things like "Your father ain't worth shit!" "He ain't worth a damn good." One of the reasons I did not see him was because my mother would not allow me to see him. It was not until my teen years that I was able to see and get to know my father.

Although I have only seen him once every blue moon, I did get a chance to know him. Cool is the one word that describes my dad. I thought my dad was cool despite all of the terrible things my mom said about him. When my dad was in prison, he earned a welding certificate. Once he was released, he found a welding job that brought in good money. I remember this part of my father's life well, because these were some of the times he gave me some of his great words of wisdom.

After getting out of prison and landing a good job, my father opened up his own business. It was a restaurant called South Shore Ice Cream Parlor. It was located on the east side of Chicago, by the beach. It was basically a fast food restaurant, a candy store, and an ice cream parlor. He bought me a bike right at the same time he opened his restaurant. This was a very expensive bike, and after two days, it got stolen from a so-called friend. This friend is now dead from attempting to stick up a dope house. My bike got stolen because I gave Darrell a ride. I gave Darrell a ride because I thought he was my friend. I gave him strict orders to go to the corner, turn around, and come right back. I watched him go to the corner, past the corner, and then out of sight.

Darrell did not live in the neighborhood. He and his family had moved out of the neighborhood about six months prior to him taking my bike. I waited all day and all night for him to come back. I was scared as hell; I did not know what to do. I knew that if I went home without that bike, I was going to get my ass kicked. I also knew that if I stayed out all night I was going to get my ass kicked. When I realized that Darrell was not coming back with my bike, the sun was coming up the next day. So I told my mom what had happened. She did not kick my ass like I thought, but she did tell me "that's what your ass get for being a hard head. Now call your no–good–ass daddy and tell him." Telling my dad was not really a problem to me because I had never seen him that much and he never disciplined me. So because of that I was not afraid to tell him. So I called him and told him what happened. My father and I looked for Darrell for two days. It would have been a waste of time to call the police because they would not have done anything. My father gave up looking but my cousin and I did not.

My cousin and I found Darrell's punk ass, but we did not find the bike. He told me that some boys jumped him and took the bike. He said he was scared to come back around the hood to tell me what happened because it was his fault that the bike was gone. Well, I believed him. It was no sense in trying to get any money from him or his mom because they were almost homeless. I told my dad what he had said. My dad looked at me like I was crazy. His words were: "and you believe him! Boy, you can't believe everything someone tells you. You need to check things out for yourself." Well I took my father's advice and checked things out. Guess what? Darrell had not told me the truth. Darrell got his ass kicked and I got my bike back.

In addition to his statement—do not believe everything someone tells you—I have also been influenced by his sayings that you should always be conscious of your surroundings, and that you must have a game plan for life. These three statements from "Dear old Dad" are the words I live by today.

Mamma Won't Take No Mess

When I was younger, I remember that it was many times that my mom woke us up in the middle of the night telling us to put our clothes on. We never had our own house. For most of my life we lived with my grandmother in a four–bedroom house. My mom was a very stubborn lady. As soon as she got mad about something, she would just get up and leave. We would go over to one of her friends' houses, my brother's dad's house, or my sister's dad's house.

My mom was a woman who did not take much bull at all. I can remember many times when mom would kick my ass for doing something wrong. Of the entire ass kickings I got from my mom, nine times out of ten I deserved what I received. My mom did not take any bull because her mother did not. As a matter of fact, none of my aunts played around when it came to respect. They were the coolest people in the world, but when it came to respect, they had to have it.

My mom and her sister were fighters, not only with life but also with people. I remember many times my aunts and my mother had actually fought with the woman next door to them. My mom was fond of telling her bragging bar–brawl stories. I remember the story that when her boyfriend at the time hit her, she kicked his ass. She took some hot water off the stove and soaked him with it, and then beat him with the pot. My mom did not take no mess.

Having It

My cousin, brother, sister, and I were the envy of the neighborhood. All the kids in the neighborhood always came to my house and played because my grandmother or mom would always give out candy, cake, or something to the other kids. We were always going to places like the circus, movies, or to the beach. People in the neighborhood thought our family had money. One reason is every new toy or big wheel that came out we got. On Christmas Day, our house looked like Toys "R" Us. Our family was no better off than any other family in the neighborhood. The only thing that made us different was that our family stuck together, no matter what. If my mom needed something, she could go to any other family member and get it, and vice versa. Looking out for each other is something that my grandmother instilled in her kids. The only thing that we had more of compared to the next family was love for one another.

The Illusion

I went to Tilden High School. Tilden was a school of three races, but mostly black. I can guess that it was about 40 percent black, 30 percent white, and 30 percent Spanish. Tilden is located on the South Side of Chicago in the middle of an all–white neighborhood. Every student there was from a so–called "low–class" family. I think there was one black male counselor who worked there.

Tilden always has had a great football team, but my class was the best. What made our team so special is that we did something that no other team in the city of Chicago had done. Despite the fact that we had to walk two miles to practices because we did not have our own field, despite the fact that most of our players played both ways (offense and defense), and despite the fact that we only had about twenty–some players on our team, we were still the first city team to win a game in the state playoffs. We did not only win a game, but we kicked ass and made it to the finals two years straight.

My mom did everything she could to straighten me out. She talked to me, prayed for me, kicked my ass when I deserved it, had her brothers kick my ass when I deserved it, and called the police to take me away when she had enough. My mom did the best that she could do with me but I was too much for her.

I thought I had it made. I was one of the captains of one of the best teams in the state. Going to class a couple of times a week—and sometimes I did not go to class at all—I still was able to play games. Teachers were passing others and me just because we put the school on the map. I also had all the girls I could ever dream of. The football players at my school got away with murder. If you were in sports, you could do almost anything you wanted. Non–athletic students that got into trouble would say, "If I were a football player I would not be sitting in this office." And they were right.

After my four years of football eligibility were up, so was the illusion that I had it made. I was so far behind that it would have taken me two more years of school, plus summer school, to graduate. I dropped out of school when my sports were finished.

The Concrete Jungle

There I was, a used–up black boy with no education and no goals. So what was I to do? After dropping out of school and realizing the situation that I was in, I tried to better myself. I tried to work, but most of the jobs I had were all bullshit jobs. Things were not working out for me, the money was not coming in fast enough, so I said, fuck it.

No education and no hope, and the dose of desire I did have was gone. This left me with the attitude, I'm going whichever way the winds take me. Living in the concrete jungle with that kind of attitude meant the other side of the law.

When I was on the football team, I often hung out with people older than me. Being in school and playing sports was one of the reasons I did not get into so much trouble. School and sports kept me away from my older friends. But when I dropped out of school, I began to hang out more with my older friends. I had all types of friends. I had friends that went to college. I had friends who were hooked on drugs. I had a friend that went to jail for a long time. I had friends that sold drugs. I had friends that were living the so–called "American Dream." I had friends that were shot down, and I also had friends that shot people down. I also had those types of friends that got fast money, faster than selling drugs. This group of friends was the group that suited me best.

You see I had no patience when it came to the things I wanted. I wanted money. Stealing was not fast enough for me. If you stole, you had to find a place to hide it, find someone to buy it, and sometimes take it to that person who was going to take it off your hands. It was just too many steps for me.

Selling drugs was hard to do in my hood at that time because police cars parked and sat in my hood, and you definitely could not go into another hood to sell drugs.

All of my friends who were the get–money–fast–friends had cars. They were always going shopping for new clothes. They were traveling to other states, seeing new things, staying in hotels, and having fun. That's what I wanted to do, the things they were doing. So I had to do the things they were doing to get the money they had to do the things they were doing.

I first started robbing people at gunpoint on the street. Most people I tried to rob––I say "tried," because we got money from the first two people, but the majority really weren't even worth stealing from. We went to robbing stores and businesses. I got good at sticking up people in these jobs; it was so easy. We would check out the spot we were going to hit, park the car a block away, walk in with masks on and our guns in our hands, do a lot of yelling, and – BAM – we're out of there (BAM meaning getting the money).

After the third robbery, it got addictive. On the seventh robbery, our minds were definitely made up; this one surely was going to be the last one. I had money, a car, and an apartment with new furniture. I was set. So why did we try to do one more – shit – I really don't know. I guess it was one of those things – the more you get, the more you want.

Love Mom

So there I was, standing inside of an Indiana courtroom, copping out for ten years and with a chance for "shock probation." My entire family was there. They stood by my side, not just from the start of this case, but from the time that I was just a thought in my mom's mind.

118

I took my family to hell and back with this case. I think I added ten years to their lives. If I would have had the smallest clues to how my wrongdoings were going to hurt them, I think I would have taken another route. My family does not have a lot of money, but they found a way to get my bond money, money for lawyers, and money to get me everything I wanted while I was locked down. I cost my family thousands of dollars.

On my left upper arm I have a tattoo of a rose. On the inside of the rose, I have the words, LOVE MOM. Often I am asked, "Why did you put LOVE MOM instead of your wife or girlfriend's name in the rose?" I say because my mom has always been there for me and always will be there for me, no matter, right or wrong.

Some of the Most Significant Events of My Life

Going to prison was the most significant event of my life. Going to prison was my wake–up call to the fact that crime is just a dead end. Going to prison was my wake–up call to the fact that I do not only hurt myself, but also people that love me and care about me. Going to prison was my wake–up call to the fact that the young Black Males are leading in all the negative aspects of American society. Going to prison was my wake–up call to the fact that a high number of Blacks are walking dead. Going to prison was my wake–up call to the fact that something has to be done to uplift the Black Male. Going to prison was my wake–up call to the fact that it is a plot by some people in society to rid itself of and stop the progress of the Black Male. Going to prison was my wake–up call to the fact that by doing what I was doing — breaking the law — I was not part of the solution, but part of the problem. Going to prison was my wake–up call.

Meeting my probation officer was a very significant event in my life. My probation officer was a young black male and was about the same age as me. He was a ladies man and a real down–to–earth person. He had experienced a lot of the same things that I had experienced. He spoke passionately about the blacks' situation here in America. He was the first authority figure that I had ever felt comfortable around. He related to me and I related to him easily. Seeing a young black male who had grown up in the same situation that I grew up in, and was doing something to help the cause, gave me the motivation to become part of the answer rather than part of the problem.

The way I decided to become part of the answer was by becoming a juvenile probation officer. By becoming a juvenile probation officer, I can get involved in youths' lives. I can be that positive "big brother figure" or "father figure" that a great number of our young blacks do not have and did not have. Becoming a juvenile probation officer will allow me the opportunity to try to influence them to stay out of the system.

CRITICAL THINKING QUESTIONS

1. What really led this juvenile into armed robbery offenses?
2. Why was imprisonment so important in turning his life around?
3. How was his relationship with his family so different than many of the stories in this book?
4. Do you think he would make a good juvenile probation officer?

15

The Life and Times of Herron Lewiel, Jr.

When I was young and growing up, I was influenced by a variety of events happening during the era. I grew up in the late sixties and seventies in a unified community called "Jew-Town" or "The Village." In this neighborhood there were projects and row houses. That means that any underground happenings a person could possibly think of could be found in this environment, and there were far too many others like it.

In this era, the most popular theme was, "Get money by any means necessary," and so there were hustlers of all shapes, forms, sizes, and styles. From stick-up men to pimps, con artists, boosters, pickpockets, and gangsters, which, when combined, elevated itself to a level of organized behavior. Our code of conduct was one and the same, and each of our struggles forced upon us a certain commonality, the forming of which came about for the sole purpose of protecting the community from outside invaders.

In this particular area, the organizations that I am able to recollect most are the Jew-Town Braves, the Jew-Town Cobras, the Mow-Mows, the Village Disciples, the Pee-Wee Village Disciples, and the Village Vice Lords.

I was introduced to the Pee-Wee Village Disciple game at a very young age. I was one of those ripe and easily impressed-upon kids that felt as if my time had come to be a part of something tough, cold-blooded, and rebellious. So I entered the stages of fashion where there was this creed that had been established by the elder groups of the community called "the belt-line." This is where each individual being inducted on that day would have to be blindfolded first; then they would be pushed through a line of others who were already members, who would stand in two single-file lines, one on each side, with belts in hand. As each person passes through, all that they would be able to feel is the welts from different belts, along with punches, slaps, and even kicks. Each of us who received this brutal punishment would be crying, but in the end, we were a part of something--a movement--something dynamically special and rebellious, a revolution; and for that, before closing, we would all have to embrace one another and shout out loud, "'Ciple!" These occurrences would take place inside of some vacant apartment that we would find, which, being in the projects, would never be a problem. To become a member of this organization back in those days, the privilege had to be earned through the status symbol of an individual's ability for toughness, hardcoreness, and secrecy in regards to whatever acts might be committed by the group.

As a group of young "Disciples," we had to form an economic base for ourselves. So we came up with the idea of a "kitty," where on a weekly basis, we would all have to put in so much money in order for us to buy clothing, weaponry, and even food. Our clothing represented a dress code of who we were, and the weaponry was for battle with others. However, back in those days, we would mainly fight with our hands, knives, chains, belts, and brass knuckles. Sometimes we would have shoot-outs with other groups, but in the end, no one on either side would be seriously wounded or dead. It was all an experience, but we each lived to see another day. The food was for either a cook-out or a meal in between school breaks.

To economically support our "kitty," we would imitate acts that we would observe being performed either by the elders of our community, or something that we saw happening in a movie on television or at the movie theater. We would involve ourselves in a variety of realms, ranging from robberies to playing the confidence game, pickpocketing, boosting, and even pimping. For instance, a typical day for us might start out by going over to a area in the hood called the "South Watermarket," which is where trucks would bring all kinds of goods or come to pick up goods and services, and we would wait. We would break into some trucks and steal case upon case of meat, drinks, and often clothes. We would then take them back to the hood and sell them. In other scenarios we would break into the trucks and steal guns, CB's, and all sorts of other items of value. Jew Town was an area that sold practically anything that a person might be shopping for, from jewelry to clothes. We would go down there on any given day and either play con and/or go in the stores and commit outright robbery. This to us was very exciting.

For example, a whole crew of us would go down to Jew Town together, but when we got there, we would pair off into groups of two. We would pick a store that only had two salespeople working. I would grab a bundle of clothes as though I was ready to purchase them, and the other brother would grab a bundle of clothes and run out of the store. One of the workers would chase the brother who left, and that was my cue to grab what I had and walk out. The clerk left in the store couldn't follow me because to do so would result in coming back to an empty store. On weekends, many of us would go down to Jew Town and get a empty TV box, fill it up with bricks stacked neatly on top of each other, tape the box up, and sell it to people as a TV. We were young, and when you're young, you don't mind taking chances. You do wild and crazy things.

Ironically, I grew up in one of those very close-knit and pretty financially stable families. My mother never lived in the area that I grew up in. In fact, she lived in a community of nothing but condominiums. However, the majority of my family did live in this neighborhood, and the underground lifestyle excited me. If there was something I wanted, all I had to do was ask my mother, and no later than the next day, I would have it. I was spoiled, no doubt about that, but I also reached a point where at a very young age, I wanted to be able to provide for my mom as well as myself. Taking things that did not rightfully belong to me at that time made me feel great. I was committing acts that made me feel good about myself.

The elders in the community would take young people under their wings and teach us things about the criminal lifestyle, and there were some that we really looked up to. One individual would have us come over to his house for a weekly lesson in the art of pimping. He would have us all take turns reading out loud from these pimp books, and then we would have a discussion group. Afterwards, he would take us out into the streets to practice. Sometimes he would even have us punish some of his own girls by placing them in the trunk of a car, and we would drive over as many bumps as we could find in the hood. When we would let them out of the trunk, they would be dizzy as heck, but it would be a very long time before we would have to do that sort of thing to them again. Sometimes we would even pour dye in their hair, or some other weird thing, but it was a trip, and it kept things in line. As I grew older and much, much wiser, what I learned from these lessons is that the best approach to disciplining the girls I would deal with would be to simply give them the choice of leaving or behaving, and it worked every time.

The elders also used the youngsters of the hood to do things for them that, had they done them themselves, they would have been severely punished by the criminal justice system—known to us as the "Just Us" system. For example, we would steal parts for their cars and they would pay us, but if we got caught, all that happened was our parents had to pick us up at the police station.

As a group of young teenagers, we became engaged in a variety of practices. Since the great bulk of our money went directly towards the purchase of fine clothing, we never had to worry about that. So every night we would participate in some kind of party, even if it just included putting a big speaker on a porch and practicing dance moves with another woman in the group. This is one of the many things that I really enjoyed, because it was like a legal pass to feel a woman's behind, or even do a split in between her legs, which in turn also presented the advantage of looking under her dress. During those days, we wore high-heeled shoes called "stacks," and some would actually have live fish inside. The shape of our collars was like a butterfly, and our brims would be sharp. We wore nothing but panamas, derbies, and Dobbs. We would also make it a point to go skating every weekend. The tripped out thing was, that even though we were out having fun, if we spotted someone to rob, then it would certainly happen.

Today, however, as I look back to what I did during these times, I think of the foolish trap that we ghetto dwellers had fallen into. Far too many of the clothes we used to wear now look like furniture coverings. The difference with me was that my clothes were made by a tailor out of silk or wool, and were always properly in style. These represented the glory years for me. Everything was going right, and the money game was out of sight. Then one of my partners got caught up in the juvenile detention process. It was partly that move that became the stepping stone for capturing me in the incarceration system.

What happened was, this friend of mine got caught in a case that sent him to a training school called St. Charles. Before sending him off though, the police told him that I was next, and they were going to make sure that I was sent away for a very long time. My friend instantly mailed me a warming letter, but by the time it arrived, I was in the same institution as he was. I was caught in one case, and on the way home from the courthouse, got caught in another.

As I was being locked up for the very first time, it really blew my mind. Instinctively I somehow knew that I just had to deal with it. I was so distraught that I could not even eat there. I will never forget what happened on my first evening there. When dinner was served, this big burly guy asked me for my potatoes. It didn't bother me so I gave them to him. Then in a heavier tone, he requested the entire tray. So I just politely looked at him and said, "This tray?" He replied with, "Yeah, give it here," and I did just that. The whole tray went right upside his head. Of course, I went directly to the hole, which is a disciplinary form of isolation where you are confined from others.

I was at this particular facility for only one month, and from there I was transferred to another called Valley View. For me, this was cool, because the institution was all about education. We had no choice but to go to school. This is where I became interested in writing. I was always reading someone else's writings, and I came to the conclusion that if others could do it, then why couldn't I. I made up my mind that I would try to do it even better.

Overall, I served exactly one and a half years there. This was quite an experience for me. While in Valley View, we inmates would have to have sessions with the institutional staff on a monthly basis to determine the progress of our behavior. They also had the authority to recommend our release. During one of these meetings, there was a teacher that I will never forget. He became very instrumental in my deep interest in the law. He told me if it were illegal processes that I was always going to be involved in, then I should consider studying the legal game. So that is exactly what I decided to do. For the remainder of my stay, I became consumed in the study of legal research. I argued and debated diligently issues of law, politics, and social scenarios. Any place I could find a mental challenge, I was there. However, what I did not know at that time, is that the legal game fell directly in sync with the art of winning people's confidence. All that it really boils down to is precisely who can tell the most convincing lie.

I would practice through letter writing, looking at myself in the mirror performing different styles, and exercising my skills on visits. Finally the day for my release arrived, and the joy I felt could not possibly be described with all the words in the dictionary. Yet, being gone for so long sprung upon me a reality shock as well, because now I had to adjust myself to a totally new world and social environment. For the first several weeks, I was constantly paranoid. I had decided to get a job, stop worrying my mother and other relatives so much, and stay out of the old environment that had gotten me into so much trouble.

I got a job as a chef at a Chicken of the Limit on the north side of Chicago. I was doing all right for myself. I had a baby on the way, but then out of the clear blue, the old habits started surfacing inside of me. I got to looking at where my employers would hide their money and would constantly be thinking about having some of my old crew stick up the place. Instead, another sort of intervention took place. I had got word that my son's mother had been saving up to get him something, and I just could not deal with something like that.

So I went back to the old hood and hooked up with my comrades, and to the currency exchange we went. We were prowling for someone to get, and finally we see this guy cashing two checks, and we just had to have him. So we followed him back to his car, and as soon as he opened the door, there I was. I was all over him, handing him blows from every direction, and I got the money while my comrade served as the watch. I suddenly heard him say, "Look up" so I did, but didn't see anyone. I continued hammering my victim until finally I saw the police running towards me on foot. I instantly broke out running, but only moments later he caught me and off to prison I went.

My partner did not go with me because I took all of the blame. The code among us during those times was that while one was serving time, the other could be out making money to support their family, and possibly yours too.

Since those years, I have served exactly twenty-two years in the Illinois Department of Corrections. One of the many things I have learned is that no matter how tough I may have thought I had it, there was always someone who had it tougher than me.

The will of Allah, and pure luck brought me out of there alive, in one piece, and even more importantly, sane. I am free now, but I still suffer greatly from the psychological trauma of trying to cope with this new society. Its deepest impact is always rearing its ugly head in my relationships. For me, there has been no one to turn to in terms of a support network. I am currently working and going to school, because I refuse to take steps backwards. I would rather be a bum living on the streets than to be buried back inside of a confined and controlled world.

I currently collect clothing for the homeless and take them directly to the shelters myself, to ensure that they are received by the needy. This is a means of reaching back to those that just simply got caught up in some bad circumstances the same as I did. Never will I forget where I came from or those that I left behind. Ironically, I am proud of my past, because it is my history, and I have no excuses. I was young and developing, and in so doing, we all make mistakes. The important thing is that I learned a lot from each of mine, and now my children and grandchildren will profit greatly from them, because I will teach and raise them to be much better.

CRITICAL THINKING QUESTIONS

1. When Herron was growing up in Chicago, what role did the gang play in his life?
2. What reason does he give for going to prison? What was the actual reason that he became involved again with crime?
3. Why is it a reality shock to return to your community after you have been locked up for a couple of years?
4. Do you believe that he has actually learned his lesson? Will he stay out of trouble in the future?

16

My Experiences as a Juvenile Delinquent

I was not the average young criminal. I am a white male, from a middle- to upper-class, two-parent home in the suburbs of a capital city in the Midwest. Both of my biological parents were (and still are) married to each other, and there was just my sister and I living at home. Mom and Dad both were extremely loving towards us kids, and while we did not get everything that we wanted, we always got what we needed. I have never seen either parent take a drink of alcohol, do a drug, or smoke a cigarette. Neither of them had ever been abusive towards us kids or each other. Neither has ever been found guilty of anything stronger than a speeding ticket. My mother stayed home and raised my sister and I, while our father went off to work every day. From all outward appearances, we were the modem version of the "Cleavers." We even had the white fence and the dog to go in it.

So how was it that from this kind and loving environment I ended up spending five years of my young life living either on the streets or in a locked institution? How was it that I ended up being permanently expelled from the local school district the first semester of my junior year, diagnosed with eight mental disorders, a chronic alcoholic/drug addict, and nearly in prison for trying to kill my own father?

And then how in the world did I end up staying sober for ten years (and counting), gaining two college degrees, one of which was from a private university--Cum Laude no less? And then why in the world did I go back into the field I had recently left as a client, only this time to be on the other side of the desk?

This is my story, the story of client 485-00-0000. I wish to remain anonymous, as my experience is no different from the thousands of youth that are currently involved in our system. We are known by our different Social Security numbers at the top of our files, but the experience is the same.

Well, I guess it all started back when I was eight or nine. I had always felt like there was a instruction book on how to live life and I had missed it. I think it was at about age eight I recalled feeling like I did not fit in anywhere. It looked like everyone I met had it together, and I did not. I don't know where this idea came from, and I guess it does not really matter now, but this feeling of isolation was very real to me, even though there was absolutely nothing to base it on. Perception is funny like that; it does not have to be real to feel real.

Like I said, I grew up in a real "normal" home. For some reason, I did not feel normal. My first major act of rebellion came when I was ten years old. I had been feeling depressed for some time prior to this event, but other than that I guess all that was out of place was that feeling of "not fitting in." What happened was, I got into a fight with my mother over something, and not wanting to deal with it, I ran away from home. It was a simple enough thing to do; I just opened up the window and jumped out of it. It seemed like the best thing to do at the time, and what happened next was completely unexpected. I felt a feeling of complete euphoria wash over me the second that my feet hit the ground. For the first time in my life I did not feel "less than," for I was doing something that I wanted to do, when I wanted to do it, knowing full well that it was "really, really wrong." The rush that I got from this new-found freedom was the best thing I had ever experienced. The feeling was so powerful, it no longer mattered to me that I was going to get into trouble. Even at that tender age, I was completely consumed with myself, and had no concern whatever that my parents may be hurt by this action. And so therein lies the microcosm of my entire life story:

Base a decision not on the facts, but on the emotions; if it hurts you, then run from it, and if it makes you feel good, then more is better. Don't ever think about how an action will affect others in your life, as they are what is standing in the way of your 'freedom."

Shortly after getting caught, I started making the rounds of child psychiatrists. I will never forget the first one I was sent to. The doctor asked me how I was feeling, and I told him, "depressed"--don't ask me how I knew what that word meant, but I did. He said, "Well, let's take a look at that." He then had me take these really long, boring tests that asked the same twenty questions fifty different ways, and just when I thought it was over, he pulls out a ton of cards with all these ink stains on them and asks me what the shapes look like. Four hours later, the doctor tells me that he will get back to my parents with the results within a week. We come back a week later, and the doctor solemnly announces to my parents, "Your son is clinically depressed." Hindsight is 20/20 and I know now that he needed to do those psychiatric assessments to determine what was going on with me. What it felt like at the time was "I told you that before the four hours of testing and week of anticipation. Did I pass it? Fail it? Am I crazy? I must be because I am the only ten-year-old I know that is depressed."

Once more I was faced with confusion and discomfort, but this time it was different. "Here is someone with a white coat and a bunch of letters after his name telling me that I am different from everyone else. Now I know why I feel like I don't fit in, because I am different, and here is my proof." It was suddenly clear to me, "talk to 'them' and get a reason to feel even more different." For the next decade, based on that emotion alone, I never trusted a thing that anyone with letters after their name said either to me or about me.

In the next two years there were a few more major blowouts, but these often revolved around school. There was a basic misunderstanding between my parents and me. They thought I should go to school and be respectful. I disagreed with them. I thought school was an extension of restrictions on my freedom, and that was the reason that my parents sent me there. Now don't ask me where I got this idea, but it was there, nonetheless. I got into arguments with kids, I stole things off the teacher's desk, even got into a couple of fights on the playground, and frankly enjoyed it. The worse I acted, the better I felt. I started making the connection that if it made adults mad, then it was fun. The more pissed they got at you, the more fun the activity had to be.

Enter the first of hundreds of family counselors. One day after getting in trouble at school, I came home and found this lady in my house sitting with my parents in the living room. They all wanted to talk. I didn't want to talk. They asked me what was wrong. I told them the truth, "I don't know." They talked to me some more. They just did not get it. The more I talked to "them" the worse I felt. I walked out the front door. My parents chased after me. They were mad, and I won the game. My only thought was, "How long before we can play again?" The only time that I ever felt in control of my life was when I was doing something to make adults' faces turn really red.

Now I was now just thirteen, and I knew what the problem was. My parents. They were the ones who did this to me. They are the ones that sent me to all of these freaks that give me labels. They were the ones who make me take these stupid pills every night. They were the reason that I am failing in school. They were the reason that I have no freedom. If only they would leave me alone to live my life the way I wanted to live it, I would be just fine. If it was not for them, I would not have to run away from home on a weekly basis. Sleeping under a bridge really sucks. The rocks make for bad pillows, and besides there is no place to set your cigarettes down without them getting muddy. But I must admit, the bridge has more freedom for me than my parents' house. I think the trade-off is worth it. If only my parents would do what I wanted them to, it would all work out just fine!

Then came an answer to my prayers. One fall day I was sitting in class--a rare event in itself--and I got called down to the counselor's office. My dad is sitting there talking to the school counselor and they have reached a decision that they wish to inform me of. I was going to be placed at a shelter for a while to "work out the problems in my family." I was elated! Finally I don't have to deal with my parents anymore! I will go to this shelter, they will see how right I am and how wrong they are, and then my parents will have to change! I could not wait to go home and pack my bags.

Dateline: November 11, 1987

For the first time in my life I have spent 24 hours in a place where I don't know anyone. The adults here are all called "staff" and we are all called "clients." The beds are hard, and my roommate--some dude I have never met--snores so loud I can't sleep. They have even more rules than my parents do, and I REALLY don't like being told what to do by people who don't even know me. The rules suck, the food sucks, and my "primary counselor" is a real bitch! She is trying to tell me that I am part of the problem, and that my parents are trying to "help" me! Does she really think that I am that dumb? I know that the only reason my parents put me here was so that someone else could control me. It was not the bad grades, or the fights we got into. No way. It was the fact that over the last few months I had been taking control of my life by sleeping on the streets instead of at home, and they did not like the fact that I was having fun.

A month later I ran away from that placement and spent the first of many Christmases on the streets. I woke up that Christmas morning leaning against a large trashcan in a back alley. I didn't mind the cold that much, as I had just stolen a carton of Marlboros from a gas station the night before. If you smoke them fast enough, you get warm.

Dateline: Mid-spring, 1988

Back at my old school. Off the streets, several pounds lighter for the experience, but it was worth it. I am now not on speaking terms with my parents--that is perfectly fine with me--and everyone at school seems to have heard about me living in that alley. These other kids are always giving me shit. Oh well, fuck them. They are just pissed because I have something that they want--Speed. I sell it in the bathrooms, and they buy it, only to bad mouth me later. My dealer and I get along great. He is a cool guy. He has a snub-nosed .357 that he lets me fire in his basement. I want to carry it, but he won't let me. I have got to figure out a way to steal it from him.

Dateline: Summer, 1988

Who the fuck turned out the lights?! One day I am in school, minding my own business, and the next thing I know I am in court! They never did catch me for selling drugs. No, they have this lady from DHS (Department of Human Services) here to lock me up. The judge is telling me all these things, but what does he know? There is something about "long-term residential treatment" and some CINA thing, and then... oh well, it is not that important anyway. I have been feeling numb inside for the last few months of my life anyway; not even running away helps anymore. I think that I should just kill myself. At least then I wouldn't have to go somewhere "long term." Who would care if I was dead anyway? Man, my life really sucks.

Dateline: Fall, 1988

I just cannot do this anymore. I hate being locked up. I hate my family. I hate my life. I have this horrid pain in my chest that never goes away. I am completely alone. No one understands me. I feel alone even when there are people in the same room. I now have three labels out of the DSM-III. Nobody I know back at my old school even knows what the DSM-III is. I do. Oh well, they are all motherfuckers anyway. I just wish that I could get out of here so I could get drunk. Last summer before I got sent to this hellhole, I got drunk for the first time and for the first time in my life I Felt Free! If I could just find a way out of here so that I could drink.

Dateline: Winter, 1988

I think I have it figured out now. Play the game. Give them behavior X, and you get "privileges." Fuckheads don't even get it; these are my rights, not my privileges. I do like some of the rights that I have, like going on home visits. Ah, home visits; translation--place to leave in the middle of the night so you can steal beer from the QT down the street. If I can get better at playing the game at this group home, then I can move up in levels and then I can actually start going out during the day without a staff member. Then I will be able to score while I am here too. Funny how all of the medications that I am on make me feel after a few beers.

Dateline: Summer, 1989

Man, am I good! I am a master at the song and dance now! I am finally out of that fucked-up place and my DHS worker is trying to get me off of paper! Dumb fucks. They don't even get it. My parents think that I am "changed." Yeah, I am changed all right. I now know that if I gain enough "trust," I can do what I want. I just have to be much more careful not to get caught. That group home was helpful in teaching me that. You had to be good to get away with shit in there. I am actually a much better con man for the experience, if you want to know the truth. Not that I care about anything anymore anyway. People are just pawns in the chess game of life. When are people going to finally realize that I am the King? I run this show, they don't. Laws are a challenge to break, not something to follow, like the stiffs that are out there. Why does everyone look so goddamn happy out here in this world? Fuck 'em. I don't care anymore. Hell, I have not cared or felt anything for almost a year now. I have been released for all of four hours now. I think it is time I go look up my old dealer and score a fifth of whiskey.

It is at this point in my story that things get really ugly. The next two years of my life were spent doing one of two things: drinking as much as I could, as fast as I could, or being locked up as a result of this drinking. I did not know that I was an alcoholic at this point in my life, but I must admit that it would not have made a difference even if I did. As a matter of fact, I think that drinking was the only thing that kept me alive through this period, even though it caused more pain than it seemed to erase. I was not interested in a long-term solution; my thoughts were about the here and now. It was during this two-year period that I was suicidal every day, and the few short hours of comfort before the blackout was worth any price. I do need to state that I don't feel that my circumstances made me into an alcoholic. I firmly believe that the reason I am an alcoholic is because I am physically allergic to it. Quite simply, when I drink alcohol, I literally "break out" in a physical craving for more alcohol. I also had a mental obsession in regard to drinking. My entire thought life was consumed with an overwhelming desire to drink, even though I knew that drinking it would get me into trouble with the law, my parents, and everyone else. This obsession told me that I could drink without consequence, even though every single experience during that two years proved the opposite. I was drinking to live. It was the only thing that provided me any source of comfort. What I know today is that drinking was a solution, not a problem. Let me explain. If I have a headache and I take an aspirin and the headache goes away, the aspirin is the solution to my problem, the headache. If my life is burning to the ground, and I get drunk to forget about it for a while, then alcohol is the solution to my pain in life. The only problem with this, of course, is that in drinking this way, one tends to create a whole larger set of problems. It was a surprisingly tough decision to make, change my entire life or die an alcoholic death.

Before I get into what my life is like today, there are two more events that I wish to relate to you. While I am going to touch on one institution in the following, the reader should know that I was in a total of fifteen of them, and the majority of those were during this two-year time frame.

Dateline: September 15, 1990

I had just come to from the night before, and once again I have no memory of the prior evening. It all fades out around 6:00 p.m. or so. Nothing new there, the last few months have been one big blur anyway. I know that I need something to drink, and there are only a few beers left in this house. I have not been home in three days, and I am sort of hungry. I may stop by for some food later. Right now, there is a chance to steal some of the beers out of the refrigerator before anyone else wakes up.

Six at night and there is no alcohol, no drugs, no nothing. I think that I will go steal some. Sure enough, a few minutes later I walk out of a store with a fifth of Jack Daniels hidden in my biker leather. I get into the getaway car, and drink this with the driver. We downed the entire thing in less than fifteen minutes. Now the buzz is on, and I have to go to another store to steal some more, as there are people back at the party who are expecting us to return with some booze. As I am leaving store number two, a 300-pound security guard convinces me ever so gently that I should not leave. The police and my dad show up, and they are not happy--I guess I win round one. I am released to my father until I stand trial for theft of the whiskey, and he says that I can't have my car back until that time. We get back to the house, and I am pissed. I have just enough alcohol in me to get started, and this fuckhead won't let me leave. Good thing I have a spare set of keys to this 1972 Olds Cutlass hidden in my Harley wallet.

I go out to start the car, and as the engine turns over, I look in the rearview mirror and see my dad's car on my bumper. With no way out of the driveway in reverse, I do the only logical thing--I drive through my neighbor's back yard to exit from his driveway. Here comes dad, running out in front of my neighbor's house on foot in an attempt to intercept me. The car dies for some reason, and as I re-started it, all of my frustration in life turned to white-hot rage. I floored it and hit my father at the same time I hit a parked car in the street at the end of the driveway. I did not know that I had hit him, as my head struck the steering wheel at the time of impact with the parked vehicle. I backed up my car to get around the car I had just hit, and heard my mother screaming "God, no!" I turned my head and saw my father lying on the street. I floored it once more and left. As I flew back to the party, I was in complete hysterics. For that ten minutes it took me to arrive back at the party I was in complete psychosis. I remember screaming in my car the entire time "Oh my God, I have just killed my father, oh my fucking God, I have just killed my father." I arrived back at the party--somehow safely--and ran inside. As I was screaming at the top of my lungs what had happened with my father, the party cleared out as everyone knew that the police would be looking for me.

Someone had shown up with beer while I was gone, and was dumb enough to not take it with them when they left, so I started drinking it. Somewhere between the third and fourth beer something very strange happened--the madness inside my head stopped. I just could not run anymore. I wanted the police to catch me. They had the house surrounded within a few minutes of my arrival, but waited three hours to come in and search it. I assume the delay was so that they could get a few warrants, one to search the house, and one to arrest me in it. When the police came to the door, I answered it. They said "Are you James ?" and I said, "Yes" and they said, "You are under arrest for the murder of your father." I was taken to jail where I spent the longest night of my life. I somehow passed out, and when I came to the next morning I found out that my father was alive, but badly injured. He was also pressing charges, and at seventeen years old I was looking at two counts of attempted vehicular homicide--felonies that would land me in prison for forty years.

I now must fast forward a little bit. After the accident, I was sent to several treatment centers in a attempt to get me sober. The only reason that I did not end up in prison was that the district attorney that was scheduled to present the case fell violently ill four hours before court, and the one that stood in was my lawyer's roommate in college. They worked out a deal with the judge two minutes before he took the bench, and I was sent to drug treatment. I simply was not ready to get sober at this time, and ended up being thrown out of all the treatment centers I was sent to. The very last place that I was sent to, prior to moving into the YMCA, was a psychiatric treatment center that dealt exclusively with conduct-disordered youth. What I am about to recount is, to the best of my knowledge, completely true. As a matter of fact, it became sworn testimony in the court case that led to the closing of the agency a few years after my placement there.

Dateline: January 15, 1991

Oh, so this is hell? I am now in the worst fucking place I have ever seen. Oh well, at least I am out of those fucking cuffs and shackles. The three-hour car ride really sucked. My Juvenile Conduct Officer is a real prick, and getting out of that car was the best thing that happened to me all day. It's not like I can leave this place now that I am here. We are on the fourth floor, and the windows can't be broken--they are triple-paned and bullet proof. The only way to access this hell-on-fucking-earth is by an elevator. The elevator has a key, and once that is activated, it goes directly to a security area where there are four armed officers on duty 24-7. Now that I am here, they are telling me stuff that is just fucked. I can't wear any of my clothing until I earn the privilege. In the meantime, I get to wear an open-backed hospital gown and paper slippers. I can not even look out the window, as that is a privilege that I must earn as well. Showers are three minutes long, and are supervised by other youths. Today it's my roommate who is supervising us. I later found out he is in here because he has been found guilty of sexually molesting 71 children--and those are just the ones he has been found guilty of; several more were pending. After the shower, they make me shave off my mustache, and throw me into the dining room. Not five minutes into dinner a youth tells staff that he won't eat the peas that are on his plate. He is taken down by six staff and placed in the control room. He is then locked in five-point restraints and left in them for 72 hours. I later found out that the staff held his dick while he pissed and wiped his ass after he shit. He was given bread and water three times a day.

Dateline: January 16, 1991

The next morning we are awakened at 5:00 a.m. Group starts at 6:30. The head psychiatrist comes in to run the group, and with this being my first group, I am the fresh meat. He starts it off by ordering me to get him a sheet of toilet paper from the adjoining bathroom. He then blew his nose into it, and made me hold the snotty rag in my closed fist for the entire group. The next hour was hell. I was screamed at by everyone present, including other residents; this behavior was strongly encouraged, and given a large notebook that I was to hang around my neck. I was to write down every single bad thought that I had while in placement in this book. I was given a Burger King crown and told that from now on I was to be called "King James," since I obviously thought that rules did not apply to me. I was then told that "I was too young to be an alcoholic," and that I "enjoyed running my father over," and that all that I was good for now was "to be a prison bitch and take dick up the ass." It got worse. They somehow knew about my being raped while living on the street by some man I did not know. My first day in group I was told that I "enjoyed it," and that it "is [my] fault for being there." I was there for 52 days.

My discharge papers said that I could not live outside of an institution without medication, that I ran an extremely high risk of both committing suicide in a vain attempt to get attention and going to prison, and that society should have me locked up, as it did not deserve to have me in the general population.

I was released from there to the YMCA back in my hometown. It was three months after my living there that I decided to go out and get drunk. I had been exposed to Alcoholics Anonymous while in treatment, but never took it seriously. I even went to a few meetings while at the YMCA, but it was more for the free coffee than anything. May 27 of 1991, I went out and got drunk. Nothing spectacular happened to me on this drunk, but I came to the next morning and for the first time in years got down on my knees and made a deal with God. It went something like this--"Okay God, if you do exist, I will go to your fucking AA meetings, do everything that they say, and in six months blow my fucking brains out, because this will not work." I was not too sure at the time about the entire heaven and hell thing. I had heard as a child that if you kill yourself, you went to hell. I wanted to make this deal with God so that when I met him--if he even existed--I could do it with a clean conscience. I could honestly look at him and say that I had tried everything, and nothing had worked. Hell has to be better than what I was going through on earth. I just wanted to cover my bases, so that when I checked myself out I could tell God that I had tried, but had to leave. I had never meant a prayer so much in my entire life. I then got up off my knees and walked two miles to the nearest AA meeting that morning. By the grace of God, I have not had a drink since.

Where my life was that day was not where I wanted it to be, to say the least. My parents had a restraining order against me, none of my friends that I drank with wanted anything to do with me, and I was a high school dropout. I was living at the YMCA, and catching the bus to a Long John Silvers fast food restaurant. I got a job there for one reason only--they were the only fast food joint I knew that had beer on tap. At night I could steal it, and nobody would know. I was homeless, more or less, and friendless. I was completely alone in a world that I knew nothing about, and the scariest part was that I knew beyond a shadow of doubt that I could not keep myself from getting locked up. My life was about to dramatically change, and I did not even know it.

Why is it that I was offered a solution to my problems multiple times in my life, only to turn it down every time? Why did I wait until I was eighteen and alone before I changed? I guess the only answer that I can provide is that I was not ready until I had run out of options. I had tried everything--I thought--to change, and nothing seemed to work. It was only after prolonged torture in the pits of alcoholic hell that I became willing to seek change. In that respect, pain is a wonderful thing. After a long enough time, it will motivate you to either change or to die by your own hand. I wish that I could offer more in the way of a solution to the reader, but my personal experience is all that I have. It has been my experience that the only way to find peace in life is to live in a relationship with a higher power of some kind. Once I commenced to live by spiritual principles, my life got better. It was just that simple. God has done for me what I was told by trained professionals was impossible to do. I live today free.

The journey that I have been on since that fateful day in May of 1991 has been nothing less than amazing. I wish that I could take credit for most of it, but, alas, I cannot. I must be honest and tell you that it is only by a relationship with God, forged by ten years of actively living the program of Alcoholics Anonymous, that I am where I am today. There is just no enough space here to recount all of the miracles that have taken place in my life over the last decade. My life has been richly blessed. I have not had to take any medications for my mental disorders since I got sober. All eight conditions have been removed from me. I show no symptoms of these disorders, and have not for several years. My parents have welcomed me back into their lives, and I now have the privilege of being a son to them. I now lay down at night with no thoughts racing through my brain. I can sit in a room with fifty people in it, and not feel alone. I can type this paper in my apartment, by myself, and not feel alone. Today, fear and resentment don't rule my life. And what a life it has been. I have climbed mountains in Colorado, swam in the Pacific Ocean, jumped out of airplanes, toured Europe, earned two college degrees, spent weeks at a time staying in monasteries on two continents, and the list of the unimpressive stuff just goes on and on. I am truly blessed to be a part of so many people's lives. I get to watch the lights come on in a person's eyes when they finally know that they don't have to live the way they had been living. I have very dear and personal friends today on three continents as a result of this. Oh this is fine, but the really impressive and biggest miracle in my life today is that I, a washed-up, burned-out, psychopathic street punk who was diagnosed as hopeless, has a active relationship with God. This is what allows me to live inside my own skin as a comfortable human being, free at last.

Today I work as a therapist with juvenile delinquents. The reason I got into this profession is simple. The night that I ran my father over, I told God that if I did not go to prison I was willing to do whatever he wanted me to do for the rest of my life. The next morning, I promptly forgot that deal. God didn't. I was about six months sober--about a year after the accident--when I received a meditation that I did not ask for. I was told that I was to work with street kids in an agency that I had opened. I thought that I had completely lost my mind. I remember thinking that maybe those psychiatrists were right after all. They weren't. I was very, very sane. From this vision that God gave to me some nine and a half years ago, my direction in life has taken purpose and shape. God and I are now within five years of making this vision a reality. The plans are on the table, and God willing, it will come to pass. I feel that the experience that I went through as a youth were for a very specific reason. I am actually very grateful for them, and given the chance, would not change a single experience. Without them, I would not have the empathy that I have for the kids that are currently in our system. I believe that we all have a purpose here in life. I was just very fortunate to have found out what mine was when I did. I look at working with kids as an honor that I truly don't deserve. Not to give the impression that they don't drive me nuts--some days, they do. It is just that to be a part of a person's life when they finally make a decision to change is a great privilege. I don't fool myself into thinking that I had much to do with it, either. I know from experience where the solution comes from--and it sure isn't me. In a way, I guess you could call me a "teacher" rather than a therapist. There is an old Chinese proverb that says "Give a man a fish, and he will eat for a day. Teach a man to fish, and he will eat forever." Today I just love to fish.

CRITICAL THINKING QUESTIONS

1. Why did this kid from a good home turn bad?

2. How did he get his life turned around?

3. With his background, what skills and experiences does he offer to the treatment of delinquents?

4. Based on his story, does rehabilitation sometimes work?

Part III

THOSE WHO ARE STILL IN PROCESS

All of these writers are in process. Two are still institutionalized. Others have been recently released from prison. All they have in common is the desire to make something of their lives.

17

A Sixteen-Year-Old Sexual Predator

My name is Andy and I am a sixteen-year-old boy from Iowa. I have one younger sister who has the same dad as me. I also have a younger brother who has a different dad. I am going to share my life to tell about how I ended up where I am today: A sixteen-year-old predator that is locked up like an animal and faces the likelihood of being on the Sexual Offender Registry for the rest of my life.

Growing up, I did not have much of a family life to speak of. I really don't remember knowing my dad. I heard stories about him being a man who drank a lot. My mom says that he used drugs too. I guess he used to get drunk and beat my mom up. She told me that he used to hurt both me and my little sister. The only memories that I have of him are when he was yelling at all of us. My dad left my mom, my sister, and me when I was about three years old. I don't care if I ever meet him because I don't know what I would do. It probably would not be good, and I don't need any more trouble in my life. From what I have heard, he was an asshole anyway.

Our family didn't have much money. I don't remember my mom ever having a job. We lived in the same apartment until I was about five years old. It had one bedroom and that is where my mom slept. I usually took turns with my sister sleeping on a mattress or on the couch. When my little brother was born he would usually sleep in my mom's bed. That apartment was always messy and dirty. I remember that my mom always had a lot of friends coming over to party. Sometimes us three kids had to sleep in the bedroom together because my mom and her friends would be drinking and playing music all night long. We had to move out of that place because we couldn't pay the rent anymore.

We moved into a house with a guy named Billy that my mom was friends with. Billy was an asshole too. He fought with my mom a lot. I can't remember how many nights I laid in bed and listened to them yell. Sometimes Billy would hit my mom and push her around the house. That made me really mad, but my mom always told me not to say anything about it because he let us live with him and that he really didn't mean to hurt her. Billy sometimes treated us kids pretty good, but when he was drinking beer, he would get mad a lot. When he got mad at us, nobody wanted to be around him. Since I was the oldest, he would usually take it out on me by throwing things at me or pushing me around. My mom would try sticking up for me, but it didn't really change anything that he did.

Sometimes Billy tried to be nice to us. He took us places and tried to be my dad. When I was about eight, Billy told me that he wanted to teach me to be a man. One night, after all the other kids went to bed, he put in a video. It was a pornographic movie that showed a guy having sex with two different women at the same time. I remember being scared and confused. I didn't understand what it was or why I was watching this. Billy told me that when a man liked a girl, he used his dick to show her how he felt. Billy made me stay up and watch those movies about once a week for a long time. A couple of times, my mom also stayed and watched them with us when she was home. Billy was always drunk when we did this. One time when Billy and my mom came home really drunk, they took off their clothes and did the same thing that the people on TV were doing. I remember Billy being on top of my mom and I was scared that he was going to hurt her. I didn't like watching them have sex, but Billy made me. That happened more and more often as I got older. I asked my mom about all of this and she said that it was just part of growing up, because that's what adults do. She always made sure to tell me that I shouldn't tell anybody.

Billy also taught me how to masturbate. He would give me magazines with naked women in them and tell me not to let my younger brother find them. I started masturbating to these magazines a couple of times a week. I never thought that any of this was different because Billy and my mom always said that it was normal. Billy and my mom would always have parties and lots of people would come over and drink and do drugs. One night this lady named Tammy took me into a room and I had my first sexual experience. She played with my penis for a while. She also showed me her tits. I was very scared and didn't know what was going on. She was very nice to me and told me that I was a very good boy. Tammy told me not to tell anybody about our little secret. She did this about three or four other nights in all, and one time she made me put my fingers inside of her. Tammy was my mom's age and I was only nine-years-old. There was one other night that I was using the bathroom and an older guy walked in. I was scared and tried to hurry up but he told me to stay there. When he touched my penis somebody started yelling in the other room, so I ran out of the bathroom. This totally freaked me out so I told my mom and she got really mad and yelled at the guy. He called me a liar and they eventually forgot about it and went back to drinking beer. I didn't realize it at the time, but all of these times I was being sexually abused. I had no idea at the time, but this abuse would be a big influence on the rest of my life.

I thought that sex was what life should be about. It wasn't so much that I enjoyed it, as it was my way to express myself and "control" others. From age eleven to age fourteen I was involved in countless sexually motivated acts. I masturbated nonstop. I stole underwear from my mom and sister so that I could masturbate in them. I touched girl's butts at recess time in school. I flashed people, showing off my body. I drew dirty pictures and wrote dirty letters and gave them to other kids. I also did things that are probably unthinkable to most of you. I played doctor with my little sister and put my finger inside of her pussy. One day when I was playing house with a neighbor girl I showed her my penis and played with her pussy. One night my mom and Billy came home drunk. My mom passed out on the couch. Billy took off her shorts and told me to fuck her, so I did for a couple minutes until he told me to move so that he could do it. I was never interested too much in boys, but one time I played with my little cousin's penis. This was all normal to me and I never saw it as a problem, just something to be quiet about.

My teachers at school must have noticed that something was different about me because they called my mom and told her that I was harassing girls at school and was making too many "naughty" comments. My mom had to come and get me from school a few times because the teachers said that I was "stalking" girls at the school. When I was thirteen I walked into a girl's house without knocking. Her parents didn't like me and they had warned me not to come over. The girl wasn't in the house and when I walked out, her parents came home and called the police. I ended up getting charged with trespassing. The judge made me do community service work.

Later that same year, I got into trouble again. I had been giving a girl dirty notes and pictures during class and she told the teacher about it. They suspended me from school. Then I started calling her house a whole lot and her parents got mad. One day after school, I followed her home and tried to talk to her. Her parents called the police and they charged me with harassment. This time I got put onto probation and had a probation officer. I also had to go see a psychiatrist. They made me go to counseling because they thought that I had some sort of mental problem. The whole time, I never told any of them about all of the stuff that I was doing.

When I turned fourteen I got into trouble again. This time it was because I had tried to kiss a girl at a party. When she tried to stop me, I grabbed her crotch. She pushed me, so I shoved her down and told her that I was going to kill her. One of the adults grabbed me and called the police. They came and took me to a juvenile detention center. I stayed there for a whole month. I never once told anybody about what I had done all the other times. When I got out, I told myself that I would not do anything to anybody any more. About two months later, I saw a girl that had been in the detention center with me. We started kissing and I tried to take her pants off. She told me not to, but I kept trying anyway. I ended up tearing her underwear and she punched me. Her mom called the police and I got locked up again. This time, they told me that I was going to get sent away for a long time. It happened, and I have not been able to walk free ever since then. That was nearly two years ago.

Since that last incident, I have been living in a locked down treatment center with other boys like me. For about the first six months, I kept everything that I had done inside of me. I was bound and determined to hide it all. Eventually, I started talking about the four times that I got into trouble with the police. As time went by, I started to talk more and more. I discovered that there were people that I could trust and they actually wanted to help me. I talked about what had happened with Billy and my mom. I talked about being abused by other adults. I talked about abusing other people. I talked about all of those things that I had promised to keep hidden. I can't tell you how good it felt to get out all of the shit that had built up for so many years. None of it was easy. I began to see that I was an animal that hurt many people. For so many years, I felt like a victim, but never realized that I was doing the same thing to others. It still doesn't make any sense that I could become a person that I hated.

The reality is that I will deal with impulses the rest of my life. I will likely be placed on the Sexual Offender Registry. For the rest of my life, people will know what I have done and will fear me and hate me for it. I have learned that there is no way of changing what has happened, but I am bound and determined to keep it from happening again. I have realized that I am a very sick person and will struggle with that illness for years to come. I wish that things could have been different. I wish that I would have had a normal life. I wish that I never would have met those bastards like Billy, Tammy, and that other guy. I wish that my mom would have loved me more and taken better care of me. Most of all, I wish that I would have made better decisions for myself and would not have hurt all those other people that I offended.

Each and every day, I hope that I will get the chance to be free again. I want to be like everyone else who can walk around in the community. I have come to hate these locked doors more than anything. My goal is to complete this treatment program within the next three months. That would be two whole years behind these doors. If I can do that, I may get the chance to return to my family and society. There is also a chance that they may still say that I am too big of a threat and likely to re-offend. I may simply be moved into another locked facility, such as the state training school, until I turn eighteen years old. Only time will tell just what my future will hold for me.

CRITICAL THINKING QUESTIONS

1. What do you think contributed to his sexual deviancy?
2. Do you believe that he belongs on a Sexual Offender Registry?
3. What do you think will happen to him?
4. If you were his treatment agent, how would you treat him?

18

I Want To Stay Out of Places Like This

I was born and brought up in Chicago, Illinois. I moved here when I was ten. I have seen a lot of stuff in my life, especially in Chicago. I have seen people get hurt and killed. In Chicago, my house was shot up a couple times.

I am fourteen-years-old, and I am now in a residential treatment program. I have been in four facilities. Two have been residential, one was a detention center, and one was a youth shelter. I have also been in a foster home.

I am here because my behavior was not that good. It all started when I was six when my step-dad had me start selling drugs for him. He didn't really care about me, and so I had to prove something to him. I have a lot of assault charges which is what brought me to this treatment program.

My father was in prison for twelve years, and my step-dad is now in prison for sixty years because he was selling drugs. The first time he was sent to prison he was on probation and house arrest when I ran away one day. He came and caught me, and he was beating on my mom. My sister called the police, and he was sent to prison. He got a sixty year sentence when he got caught selling crack cocaine.

My mom and all of us live with my auntie, and I can't go home on a home visit because she lives with my auntie, and we don't have our own house. My auntie is actually on probation, and my probation officer doesn't want me to be around her. She has a son on probation and another one of her sons is in prison.

I didn't like school that much because I didn't know too much about it. I didn't know how to read or write. I still don't care that much for school. My mom would try to make me go, but I would ditch that idea and take off.

I was in a gang. I was a GD [Gangster Disciple] and didn't hang out with others in rival gangs. I got into a lot of fights because I was in a gang. What I did for the gang was sell drugs for them. I stole stuff for them, too. I also dealt with their problems. If anyone had a problem with anyone, we would go and fight the person that he had a problem with. We would jump them. I was jumped a couple times, and sometimes they got back at me.

I was actually in the gang my step-dad was in, and sometimes when we were in a block selling drugs, we would be shot at. We had a basement, and he kept me watching his drugs in the basement. Other gangs would shoot up our house sometimes. My mom got tired of it and moved us out of Chicago.

I wanted to be in my own gang, so I started a gang of my own. I was still a GD and would fight BDs. I have a lot of enemies.

We were walking home from school when I was twelve. I was with one of my cousins, and we had gone back to Chicago for a while. We saw a bunch of people. They were older than us, and they started to dis us. My step-dad told me that I would be stupid not to walk around with a gun, and so he gave me a gun. He gave me a nine millimeter, just for protection.

I thought that my mom didn't care about us, because she was rarely home. I have seven brothers and sisters. I have one brother in training school, but I don't talk much to him.

My mom used to smoke weed around us a lot. She never did cocaine or nothing. She really didn't know that my step-dad was selling cocaine. I thought she had a drinking problem because she would get drunk and not come home. She would dismiss me, and she wouldn't want me or any of her kids around.

She quit drinking, and she quit doing weed. She quit doing everything, but we still have our problems though.

This is going to be the last facility I am going to be in because I want to go home in a couple months. I have spent two of my birthdays in facilities, and I have missed out on two birthdays. I have spent one here.

Another one of my summers is when my mom was in her "I don't care moods," and it was my birthday but I stayed around watching TV all day. It felt just like a regular day. That was when I turned twelve.

My goal is to get out of placement and to actually do right because I have brothers and sisters. I do not want to see them go to placements, like I have.

I can't say that people have made any difference in my life. The person who made the difference is me. I actually decided to choose my path. I was walking down the wrong path. I decided to get off that road.

CRITICAL THINKING QUESTIONS

1. This fourteen-year-old young man has seen a lot in his few short years. What impact would these experiences have on a young person?

2. He clearly has a rough road in front of him. What is needed in his life, beyond his resolve, to turn things around?

3. What obstacles does he face in his life at the present time?

4. What strengths does he have?

5. His mother seems to move the family back and forth to Chicago. How much support does she actually provide for her family? Is she likely to be a more responsive mother now that she is no longer drinking or smoking marijuana?

6. What impact would it have on a young person's life to be given the task of selling drugs for his step-dad at the age of six?

7. This young man has all kinds of family members in prison – his natural father, his step-father, and his aunt's one boy. He also has a brother in training school. How much influence would this family history of incarceration have on a young boy?

19

A Juvenile Drug Dealer

My life didn't really take a turn for the worse until I got my first job. I moved to the Midwest when I was thirteen years old, and I got my first job when I was fifteen. For most people getting a job is really exciting, and for me it wasn't any different. I loved my job, and the people I worked with were really cool, and later I found out that they were pretty heavy drug users.

At the time I was living out in the suburbs in a wealthy part of town. My parents had a good job, we had a very comfortable home, and I wasn't really in want of anything. As I started working, I began working only a few hours every week, so there wasn't much time for me to be influenced by the actions of my coworkers. When I turned sixteen I was allowed to work a lot more hours every week, and work a lot later at night. It was not unusual for me to put in at least 40 hours a week and be at work until two or three in the morning. When I worked late at night I met a lot of the friends of my coworkers, and it wasn't unusual for us to go back in the cooler and smoke weed every day. As I got used to smoking weed, I started hanging out with my coworkers away from work, and while doing this, I was exposed to lots of drugs. Over the course of a few months I went from just smoking pot to drinking heavily, smoking heavily, doing acid, and the occasional line of coke.

My job was paying me very well, so at first I could easily afford all of my drug use. When I started using more and more, I realized that I was running out of money, so I became a drug dealer. I started out just hooking up my friends, and by the time I was finished, the vast majority of a small city was coming to me and going through me. I was making an incredible amount of money and most of the drugs were going directly through the restaurant that I was working at. For example, someone would come through the drive-through and order a certain food item. When they pulled through, they would pay for and receive a specified amount of drugs. It was normal to make a few thousand dollars during a shift. With all of the money coming in, I never really thought that this wasn't the life I was raised for. I had parents who took care of me, yet had no idea of what I had become. My drug dealing game went on for months, until one day at school someone took it upon themselves to go and tell a teacher that they suspected me of being a drug dealer. At this point I was searched by authorities and the police were called. All I had on me was about a half ounce of weed and about five hundred dollars, but it was enough to get me charged with possession and with intent to deliver a controlled substance. It was kind of a wake-up call for the school. They had tried to picture themselves as a perfect little community and never imagined that a kid such as myself was capable of running a business on their own premises. They kicked me out immediately. I was placed on probation by the juvenile court. I was pretty lucky to get probation, because the other option was being locked up until I turned eighteen.

My crimes were also a huge shock to the community that I live in. They had been under a misconception that such things don't happen in such a nice, white suburban community. In reality, I was just a small player in a much bigger picture. I have since quit using and selling, but I am sure that someone else simply stepped in where I left off. As far as my future goes, I have set new goals and will reach all of them without drugs. The hardest part will probably be knowing the fact that I could make easy money in a heartbeat if I want to. I just need to remember what I have always known, and that is the values and morals that my parents taught me.

CRITICAL THINKING QUESTIONS

1. Why did this young man begin to use drugs?
2. How did he go from a user to a dealer?
3. Will it be easy for him to stay away from drugs when he is released from his present institutionalization?

20

A Sad Story

My name at birth was Antonio Marcus Harrington. I was born in Waterloo, Iowa on August 4, 1970. My parents and I spent a short time living across the street from my maternal grandmother and my step-grandfather. After a couple of months my father, mother, and I moved to Rockford, Illinois.

My father was into various criminal enterprises, among them pimping and selling drugs. He was quite a womanizer, and this naturally led to problems with his wife, my mother. She attempted to leave him and came home to Waterloo; however, her mother and stepfather made the mistake of urging her to return and try to work it out with her husband.

It did not work out and her discontent may have led her to make a fatal choice. She indulged in adultery, perhaps with the thought of "what's good for the goose." Unfortunately, infidelity is neither good for the goose nor the gander, especially when a violent goose with a very short temper catches you.

My mother was caught in the act with me present. There were shots fired, and in the aftermath I lost a mother. My grandmother lost a daughter, my aunts and uncles lost a sister, and my mother lost her life.

This is my original wound. We all have one wound; it has left me very non-trusting of most people. My maternal grandmother and her husband brought me back to Waterloo. After my father went to prison, he relinquished his parental rights in order to allow my adoption by my grandparents.

I was eighteen months old when my name became what it is today, Antonio Marcus Johnson. It was not simply a change of name, but of destiny. Two very wonderful and excellent people who were devoted to God, family, and society raised me. My grandmother worked for the school system for over twenty years, and my grandfather worked for John Deere, the University of Northern Iowa, and Viking Pump, all very good jobs.

I was sent to Northern University High School, which is an excellent school. I was a nerd and a jock rolled into one. I did well in school, all As and Bs without much effort. I got one C in industrial tech in ninth grade.

Living with my grandparents, we naturally attended church. However, we did not just attend; we were involved from top to bottom, start to finish. I went to Sunday school and church every Sunday. I served as an usher, sang in the choir, went to Sunday school conventions as a delegate. I was in the Young Peoples Department and a delegate to the conventions. I went to a church camp called Camp Baker in Michigan. I read the 25 articles of religion for the Founders' Day Banquet when I was around twelve years old.

Since third grade, I always wanted to be in some sort of federal law enforcement. My favorite TV shows were all cop shows with guys like Ken Walak and the Duke. My other favorites included science fiction--I am a Star Trek fan--and mythology.

In junior high I did independent studies on those subjects that piqued my interest. I would go to the school library and borrow the Iowa code and go down to the copy room and copy sections from the Criminal Code: murder, robbery, rape, assault, drugs, etc. I wanted to fight it all. I also read every book I could find on astronomy, astrology, and mythology. I understood my motivation for law enforcement. I wanted to try to save as many people as I could from suffering a wound from crime the way I did.

It was only after going to prison and thoroughly studying society, religion, and myself that I finally understand why I always loved law, astronomy and astrology, and mythology. What Western man calls religion is made of all these elements, as well as social customs, ethics, etc. I did almost everything in church except preaching the message, yet I really didn't like being there. There was so much I did not agree with.

All my life I have been a very good athlete. I played football, basketball, and track and did very well in them. We won Class 2-A State Track four times in a row. I ran as a freshman; my senior year we got State Runner-Up in basketball. I was All-State in track and still have the school record in the 100-meter dash. If I had taken sports more seriously and had been willing to give 200 percent, I probably would have gone on to play basketball and football in college.

I graduated with a 3.5 grade point average from high school and went right to college summer school at Luther. I started at Luther in the fall, and my first semester there, I got into trouble playing with a white female. I had a fake gun and showed it to her. Immediately the question was raised: "Is it real?" My response was, No, and let me show you that it is harmless." I showed her that the plastic trigger could not be pulled, that there was no real danger, and that I intended her no harm.

We got to playing around, and that is when I got into trouble. She had hit me lightly in fun. I responded, and foolishly played too rough. Instead of letting this go, she took it to the administration. A few days later, I was served with papers concerning assault.

That incident caused me to give up my life-long law enforcement dream and to put my future up in the air. I was suspended for two weeks for having a BB gun and bad judgment. I went home, transferred to the University of Northern Iowa, and majored in criminology. I was considering a career in probation/parole.

I still cannot understand why whites, who have a terrible history with violence, including genocide, slavery, lynching, etc., fear every dark face in the world. Yet it is they who have done the worst violence in the world. I learned a lesson though. I was foolish for even playing with a gun--real, or not--and more foolish for playing with her-- classmate, or not.

It was another classmate at UNI, another white female, who would aid in the ruin of much of my life. I helped her destroy me so she could get a career with the Drug Enforcement Agency started.

During my childhood, I was so honest that at twelve years old, I told my cousin not to steal a two-cent piece of gum. I informed him that if I saw him, it would be my civic duty to turn him in. I went from this position to that of being the city's most wanted drug dealer.

When I was looking for a job during the period in between leaving Luther and going to the University of Northern Iowa, I was turned down for every single job. I refused to live off my grandparents or on the state, so I decided there was only one way I could pay the bills and be a good, all-American materialist. I went to see the equal opportunity employers on the corner and started selling drugs. I had no intention of making a life of it and intended to stay in school.

I really never felt comfortable with being a drug dealer, and I always wanted a feasible way out. Yet at the time, I couldn't seem to find it. I got caught once, then I became a young black male with a felony record. So, now what was twice as hard, became three times as hard. I was spending too much time on the street and out-of-state to pay full attention to my studies.

When I first started selling dope, I was so out of place that I took my criminology textbooks to the park and bar, to sell dope and study at the same time. I finally was academically suspended because I let my grades suffer too much.

Before I was suspended, I was taking a class called the Sociology of Policing." It was in this class I met Sandy Bums, who did all she could to destroy my life and to advance her career. She would justify her actions by saying that what she did was to stop a vicious dope dealer and to save children.

However, I have never used violence. Nor have I ever sold dope to children. I am the first person to admit that what I did was wrong. I believe everyone should receive justice. I believe that the punishment should fit the crime, which is the basis of an eye-for-an-eye philosophy.

Yet I do not believe in planting weeds so they can be pulled, and then being called a master gardener for doing it. After developing a friendship, she and I spoke about the drug business. I never glorified it; I only spoke about it.

So they did not hear on tape what they really wanted to hear. She asked about violence; my reply was that it is foolish and brings more scrutiny from law enforcement. So now the question, have you ever sold drugs to children? I responded in the negative. A child may steal $5 to $20 from a money purse just before the hammer drops. It just doesn't make sense to fool with children.

I then went on to speak in monetary terms about selling drugs. Those who sell dope are 99.9 percent in it for the money. The goal is to make as much money as possible in the shortest amount of time while avoiding prison for the longest period. The best customer is a man with a great job or other dope dealers so that money is made in the hundreds and thousands of dollars.

I was not all bitter about being caught and punished, because I did wrong and I realize my role and my own wrongdoing. It was my choice to get involved, and I chose to allow myself to be pulled into the fire. I pled guilty, though there was no good recording, no marked money, and no hand-to-hand transfer of drugs. It would have been her word against mine.

When I arrived at her apartment, she was there with the money to buy drugs, all ready. I came only with myself and I accept my responsibility. I have never tried to coax a person into selling drugs, and at times I attempted to discourage people from buying drugs.

At the time, all I wanted was to go back to a normal life because it isn't worth the loss and pain. I used to walk at the Dome in which our high school played home football games and we ran track meets there. I shed tears wondering how I had allowed myself to fall into such a terrible position. I wished for a way out that still paid the bills.

Selling dope and using dope are addictive. Using dope stays in the blood and disrupts the brain and travels in the blood so it becomes your life. This is the answer to all who say, "Well why didn't you just quit or stop?" I ask all you drunks and smokers--why don't you just quit?

My only justification is that I only dealt with people who were already involved. I told Sandy that, and that I didn't understand why she would want to get involved. When someone used to tell me they quit, I never tried to coax them back into it. I would always shake a hand and give a hug and tell them I truly hope they stay away from that garbage. It really isn't for everyone.

So why did I stay in after telling others that? Probably for the same reason that Jimmy Swaggart is caught in hotels with women. Sometimes, for worldly motive, we act against what we know to be right. I was addicted and had not found the strength to break away. When I finally did, I had the misfortune of meeting the wrong person and being in the wrong place at the wrong time. I received three times the amount of time most people get for the same crime.

I was eventually arrested for what I allowed Sandy to coax me into. They had been following my family and me all the way to Indiana hoping and praying that I was going to get more dope, but this never happened. All I wanted to do was to go back to school and get my life back on track. If minorities are on track, it seems to me that every effort is made to derail them.

I went to court, pled guilty, and found out, to my surprise, I faced 112 years because of a prior drug conviction. So I faced 25 times three, and minor drugs, all adding up to 112 years. The probation officer who did the sentence investigation report recommended the maximum sentence. The judge heard all I had to say, then took his earplugs out and spoke. He said, "I am inclined to believe much of what you have said here today. I believe that had you been sent to prison the first time I don't believe you would have committed any further crimes. Furthermore, I believe had law enforcement not pursued you so vigorously, I don't believe you would have committed this crime."

However, then came the fatal blow. He said the law had changed. If I had been charged for the same crime a year, or even a few months prior, I would have only gotten ten years, but now I could get 25. He also said because of a past offense it could be doubled or tripled. He said that had I not pled guilty, I would have gotten the whole 112 years, but since I took responsibility, he was only going to double the 25 to 50.

I got the same time as a second-degree murderer, with a longer mandatory minimum than a person who kills another. No man in his right mind could ever compare a non-violent crime in which no one is forced to do anything to the taking of life.

I was a captive of the system for nearly ten years. Many may foolishly say, "Well you did the crime," and yes, I did - and I did my prison time. I became a Muslim in prison, and it has changed my life.

It is not so amazing that I got into trouble even with a good stable home, church, Boy Scouts, Upward Bound, college prep, and FBI aspirations. What I find more interesting is that materialism is too often promoted in this society, and spirituality is ridiculed. If this continues to be the modern Babylon, it will self-destruct,

I am currently working at a tannery, hoping one day to be in a position to help every Black, Latin, Native American child in this country to have a computer in their home. I want to find a way to help oppressed peoples, so crime is not the only way they seek to survive.

I am now married and recently I became a father for the first time, at the age of thirty. Life is still a struggle, but I am making it, and I intend to stay as relatively free as I can.

CRITICAL THINKING QUESTIONS

1. Why did this young man with so much promise go wrong?

2. What was the real attraction in selling drugs for him?

3. Does he seem to be embittered by his experiences with the system?

4. What did you learn about drug-trafficking from this story?

Part IV

THOSE WHO HAVE GONE ON TO ADULT CRIME

The stories in this section are sad stories. These individuals are still in prison. Most of them committed violent crimes, either as juveniles or adults, and all of them have a history of delinquent acts during their juvenile years. In addition to their present predicament, the discerning reader will also discover that other events in their childhood were usually quite different from the other stories in this book.

21

The Thinker

Who am I?

I have asked myself that question many times. I still don't know the answer. At twenty-five, I'm not sure I'll ever know, so it would probably be best if I told you who I used to be. Perhaps, that will give you some idea of who I am.

I was born the older twin boy of identical twins. My mother was a young mother, nineteen when we were born. My father was in his late twenties and on his third marriage. He wouldn't be in the picture long.

My life started as a struggle. My brother and I were born three months premature and spent several weeks in incubators before being allowed to leave the hospital. Life has continued to be a struggle up to the present. My brother and I are both serving life sentences in state prison for murder.

However, life has not all been bad. My brother and I have always been close, and we did everything together as kids. I understand him on a level that someone who is not a twin would not be able to understand. I've always had someone to love, and I've always been loved. I am truly blessed with our relationship.

Were we bad kids? I don't believe we were. We just went wrong at the right time! Products of our environment? Possibly?

I've gone from beginning to end. Now, let me fill in the middle.

Early Years

My mother and father had separated and divorced when my brother and I were about one and a half. It was documented that we were sexually, physically, and psychologically abused when we spent weekends with our father on shared custody visits. At two and a half, we were supposedly sexually abused [anal sodomy], but I don't remember that.

I also don't remember the physical abuse, but it was the physical abuse that brought attention to the sexual abuse. On one visit, my brother and I were both supposed to have "fallen" off our tricycles and broken our front teeth. Not just our two front teeth but rather all our front teeth. For the next six years, the front of our mouths were filled with silver caps until our adult teeth grew in and the old ones fell out.

One thing I do remember from the first couple years (actually, my earliest memory) is that I had soiled my underwear. I remember I was terrified of what my father would do to me. My brother and I hid the soiled underwear in a small hole in the bathroom wall. It was about a foot off the floor and behind the door. I don't know how my father found them, probably the smell, but when he did, he made my brother and me stand with our backs to the wall. He turned the underwear inside out and held the feces up to our faces. He said, "Do you see this? If either one of you do this again, you'll eat it! Do you understand me?"

Finally, my mother managed to get sole custody of my brother and me, and we didn't see our father again for another six years.

My mother got pregnant again and had my sister about two months before our third birthday.

My sister never knew her dad. He left before she was ever born. She had a lot of problems dealing with this later on when she got older. My mother was never married to my sister's father; he was just a boyfriend. I don't remember him at all, so he probably was not around long.

My mother would marry again and again and again. At last count, she has married eleven times. My mother has a lot of psychological and emotional issues. These problems would manifest themselves over the years, but at the time I knew nothing about these kinds of problems. I didn't know why my mother would spend hours in her room crying, or how she could be happy and playful one minute, and then be angry and mean the next. As an adult, I understand her problems, and I see them for what they are. She still exhibits the same patterns of behavior and completely denies anything is wrong with her.

My mother is a bipolar borderline manic depressive. Most of the time she doesn't really fully grasp the long-term consequences of her actions. She functions off her immediate feelings and how she feels at the moment. Sometimes she reminds me of an adult teenager who can't think past the moment. There are times when she's able to function perfectly, but most of her decisions are impulsive. Emotionally, she detaches from feelings that are uncomfortable or she'll dwell on them until they overwhelm her.

My grandmother was always like a second mother, almost a replacement for a father. Over the years, we lived with my grandmother many times; her house will always be home to me. My mom would get married and we'd move; she'd split up and we'd move back. Sometimes, even when she had a new husband, we'd find ourselves living with Grandma.

Some of the greatest memories I have are in her house. When my mother wasn't there or when she was alone in her room, Grandma was always there to entertain and look after us. Later, when I reached adolescence, she was the one who caught the brunt of our rebellion.

Shortly after my sister was born, my mother met my first stepfather. They got married when I was four. We moved to a small town about an hour and a half from my home town. I remember living in two different houses with them. The first house was small, a one-story house with a small backyard. The neighbors had kids of their own. I don't remember them much, but I know they had a couple of daughters and maybe one or two boys who were all a little older than we were. They had an older daughter who I had a huge crush on. I believe it was my first crush.

I remember my mother and my stepfather arguing, but not a lot at first. We had a small basement where we would ride our tricycles. After a while, I was afraid to be down there, probably because they chose to fight in that area. To a child of four, when your parents fight every time they go down into the basement, you start to think the basement is the cause of their fights.

My mother broke her foot on the back porch steps. It wasn't long after her foot was broken that the fighting really started again. They stopped trying to hide it after awhile, and the fighting became more frequent. By the time winter came, they weren't speaking much. She left not long after that, and we moved back to my grandmother's house. They got a divorce and that was the end of stepdad number one.

My grandmother was married, her fifth, to a guy who was really good with us. He was like a pseudo-father! We idolized him! I remember he had his favorite chair in the living room. It was box-shaped, big and square, with large arm rests. That is where we always sat, one on each side.

I have a lot of really good memories of my step-grandfather. Everything was like a big adventure with him. He was our first real role model! He introduced my brother and me to the forest that was about a quarter mile from my grandmother's house. Later that forest became like a sanctuary, our own personal never-never land with one adventure after the next.

We had turned five the previous fall, so come September we started kindergarten. Our school only had half-day classes for kindergarten, so we got home around 11:30 in the morning. He was always waiting for us with macaroni and cheese with hot dogs cut up in it, grilled cheese sandwiches, or soup.

After we ate, he would have something planned for us to do, like walking in the woods. He always had a lesson for us, such as "This is good! This is bad! Don't touch this. You can find this here!" He would make us stuff to do. He cut small branches and used twine to make us bow and arrows. Nothing dangerous - the arrows would only travel about twenty feet. We still thought they were the coolest things ever. He made us slingshots, wooden toy guns, and many other things. I could a fill a book on just the memories I have of him, and all this took place in a six-month stretch of time. Before our sixth birthday, he would be gone.

My mother didn't like my step-grandfather. She thought he was a freeloader, lazy and living off my grandmother. He didn't work, and my grandmother was the breadwinner of the two. To my mother this was reason enough to start arguments with him. She would find something to fault him on and then turn it into a big issue. As time passed, she found more and more to fight about. Finally, one day in early fall, she gave my grandmother an ultimatum. It was either her and the kids, or him. Grandma chose us, and he left.

The following year my mother met and married my second stepfather. He was a couple of years younger than her, and his family did not like my mother much. Soon, we were moving again - this time to his home town. We stayed about three days and moved back. My mother said she didn't like living there because the neighborhood scared her. Their marriage lasted a month or so longer and it was over.

170

Before long, my mother began seeing someone new and in no time they were married. Insert stepfather number three. He worked during the afternoon, so we didn't see him much. By winter, they had started fighting on a regular basis. I can't remember the source of the arguing but after awhile it was very uncomfortable for the two of them to be around each other. Thus, stepfather number three was history.

We moved into a small trailer on the west side of town and stayed there for a month or two. Finally, when money got tight, it was back to living with Grandma. The rest of the school year wound down, and I finished my first grade year. Summer came and we stayed with Grandma.

My mother, now single and in her mid-twenties, sowed a few wild oats. She spent a lot of time dating and going out to bars. Grandma babysat us quite a bit during this time frame. That summer we signed up for Little League Baseball. Not having a father to teach us the game, we weren't very good. I had to hit the ball off of the T-stand my first couple of games, which was quite an embarrassment. We got Grandma to help us practice in the field next to her house. She had a bad shoulder, so she had to pitch to us underhanded. My hitting improved enough that I didn't have to use the T any more. I still wasn't very good. I was jealous of all the kids with dads. I felt inferior to them.

My mother met another guy at the end of summer, and you guessed it, married him not long after. Stepfather number four didn't spend much time with us. I remember his parents were dairy farmers. We went to their farm once; we watched a movie while we were there. I've got a pretty clear memory of that day. It's funny the things we remember!

My mother had a job at this time. I don't remember where she worked, but she didn't get home until a couple of hours after we got home from school. The stepfather was there but mostly stayed in bed during this time of day. He had a night job somewhere.

My grandmother didn't like him, and it didn't take long for her dislike to intensify. He had a stash of porno magazines hidden in his bedroom kept between the box spring and mattress. While we were at school and mom was at work, he had time alone with his smut books. Kids snoop, and it didn't take us long to find them.

With mom working days and his working nights, they didn't see each other often. I don't remember them fighting much, but it didn't take long for it to end. We hadn't ever moved when mom married that time. Our stepfather had been staying at Grandma's house the whole time so my life wasn't really affected by his leaving. By now the stepfather leaving was just part of our growing up.

My mother let us get a dog not long after he was gone. I thought of the name "Sugar."

We had a dog before Sugar, but it got poisoned and we weren't very attached to it. We didn't really miss it when it was gone. Sugar was different. She was like a member of the family. My grandmother was allergic to dogs and cats, so Sugar stayed in a dog house under our backyard deck.

My brother and I had turned eight that fall and were in the second grade. We were still getting by on our grades, but by now our teachers had some concerns about us not completing homework assignments. This pattern of concern would continue.

The school year went by, and we were getting close to summer break. It was near the beginning of April 1987 that my mother got a phone call from an attorney one day. He said that my father had contacted him and was asking for visitations with my brother and me. My mother was for some reason concerned that if she said no, they would fight for full custody, so she agreed to every other weekend.

The following weekend we packed our backpacks with clothes and a couple of toys and readied ourselves for our visit with our father. He was now remarried to a nice woman named Janice or something close to that.

I had this image in my head that my visit was going to be a nightmare, some torturous event, but for the most part we had a lot of fun. We played and watched movies on TV and had pancakes for breakfast. It wasn't traumatic or anything. So two weeks later when he came to get us for a second visit, we were looking forward to going. Kids are quite forgiving and forget easily.

When the time came for our third visit, he called and said he wasn't going to get us, nor would he be back to get us for anymore visits. We never saw him again.

My mother doesn't know how to show her love for her mother. She is always relying on her for help, but she doesn't really seem grateful. She finds little things to harp

172

on and nitpick at. She still complains about the things Grandma does. They seem very insignificant to me, but to Mom they are great annoyances and unbearable problems.

We turned nine that fall and started the third grade, but before the fall came we moved to a little trailer in a little trailer park. My mom said that she couldn't bear to live at Grandma's any longer. My mom didn't have a job then, and we lived on public assistance. I remember Mom sold our bikes for extra money.

Right about that time my grades started to get bad. I couldn't concentrate. I was bored. I was always daydreaming and asking to go to the bathroom, anything but my class work. I stopped doing my homework. Even when I tried, I couldn't concentrate for long. I was lectured and told to do better, but I just continued to do more of the same. I was lucky to receive a passing grade that year.

My mom decided to bake my brother a cake because he had done well on a test or his report card. While the cake was cooling, the mice we lived with helped themselves. Mom decided that was enough of that, and we moved back to Grandma's.

That summer my mom started dating a neighbor guy. I started the fourth grade still living with Grandma, but it wasn't long before mom had brought the idea of marriage to the table. Enter stepdad number five. We moved in with him later that fall. This was probably the most normal family life I experienced during my childhood.

Later that year my stepdad filed a petition to adopt my brother, sister, and me. The following summer his petition was granted, and we took on his last name. My brother changed his first name as well because his name was also the name of our biological father.

We had a good life for three years. I have hundreds of good memories from this time in my life. We went on vacations; had big Christmases; had a swimming pool, pet dogs, ducks, geese, rabbits, and chickens; and we were twenty yards from a forest we loved. Life was great!

The summer when we were ten, my brother met a girl at the skating rink. Not having a girlfriend of my own, I got hooked up with her younger sister who was my age. I had my first kiss and many to follow with my girlfriend.

<u>Middle School Years</u>

My fourth grade year was not much better than my third. I would struggle to pay attention and got bored easily. I didn't have enough credits to pass, so I had to go to summer school. My brother was having the same troubles as I was having, so he went to summer school right along side me. We turned eleven and started fifth grade. We were placed into remedial reading classes because our reading skills were behind. Our grades were not good, but we did pass.

There weren't many fights between my mom and new dad. I realized early that this was because when Mom would pick a fight, he would just ignore her. When problems between them increased and he became more distant, my mother insisted they go to counseling to fix their problems. My new dad had some serious issues from his childhood that made him emotionally distant. He kept everything inside, and it had been eating at him for years. He vented some of his issues at these sessions, and even expressed that at times he had a desire "end it all." He told my mother on their way back from one of these sessions when she was picking on him, that he "felt" like pulling the jeep out in front of a semi-truck and killing them both. They stopped going, probably because my mother didn't trust his driving any more.

That summer we also got our first real guns. My brother got a .22 rifle that had been our dad's. I also had a .22 bought for me. My gun had a plastic stock and barrel, made for a young shooter and easy to carry. We'd go squirrel hunting and target shooting. I got pretty good at shooting.

We started the sixth grade and turned twelve. I am not sure of the reasons why but that fall we moved back in with Grandma. I think my mom and stepfather had gotten spending-happy and got in debt. They fought a lot while they were at Grandma's. It was usually one-sided. My dad would just sit there silently ignoring her and letting it build up.

One cold February morning I heard screaming. My mother was screaming, "Help? Help!" I ran into their bed room. My stepdad was beating my mother. He had her by the hair and was throwing her around. I grabbed my trusty .22, which was not loaded, and pointed it at my stepdad. I told him to stop or I'd shoot him. He turned his attention to me. He grabbed my gun and yanked it from my hands. He knocked me to the floor with the stock and began to beat me with the butt of the gun.

My mother jumped on his back and got a hold of the gun. I managed to get up and leave the room. My sister was in the hall crying. My brother, who had seen me getting beat, took my cousin who had been spending the night and ran bare foot in shorts and no shirt a mile to the neighbor's house. My sister and I started to do the same, but before we reached the end of the driveway, my mother ran out of the house and called us back. She took us into a room, just off from the den, to have us put on our shoes while she went to get the truck keys.

My mother came back with the keys. We filed into the truck and went to get my brother and cousin. We drove to the hospital, and I got a few stitches and bandages here and there. My brother was all torn up because he thought he should have done more to help. My sister just kept crying.

The sheriff went out to get my stepdad, who had laid out some guns and ammo, for what I'm still not sure - either to kill us, himself, or to shoot it out with the cops. He never used them and went easily into the cop's car. That night and the next day, we stayed at a safehouse, which was probably unnecessary because my dad spent the next twenty days in jail.

I never really blamed him or hated him. I even missed him when everything was all over. We had two supervised visits and then I didn't see him anymore.

I went to school with bandages all over me, and I got to answer all the questions and explain what happened. I acted tough, but I wanted to cry. I don't know why, but I felt ashamed. I was glad when the bandages came off. I failed that year and summer school wasn't enough to make it to the seventh grade. My brother failed, too.

That summer my mom met another guy. He was about seventeen years older than her and had two grown sons. By the end of the summer, they were married, and we were moving into his house. Enter stepdad number six. A month or so later he had a mid-life crisis and told my mom he wanted to split up. So, we moved out, back to Grandma's.

About a week later, my mother got drunk and gave him a phone call to talk things out. He said it was over, and she lost it. I heard her scream and throw the phone across the room. I went to see if she was all right and she screamed at me to get out. So I did.

She screamed and cried for a while and put her dresser in front of the door so we couldn't get in. We couldn't see what was going on in the room. Then she broke the picture frame that had his picture in it, held it to her neck and throat, and said she was going to kill herself.

One of us called our social worker, the one assigned after the beating. She came out to the house. She managed to get the bedroom door open more and to talk with mom. The social worker was able to calm her down some. The sheriff and deputies showed up, and when they found out she had made threats to kill herself, they decided to arrest her and take her to a mental health hospital for observation. They drove her five hours to the other side of the state to admit her to the state psychiatric hospital. They kept her for about five days, and then we drove down to get her. It was a long drive.

A few weeks later stepdad six came to see mom, and they seemed to work out all their issues and decided to get back together. We moved back in together and everything was good for a while. Toward the end of summer, my new stepdad got transferred to a really small town in order to run one of the auto parts store franchises. It was about two hours away from Grandma's house.

The town wasn't that bad. We made some great friends. I've got a lot of great memories from the six months we lived there. I felt free there. I could come and go as I pleased. We turned thirteen and started our second year of sixth grade. I got a new bike for my thirteenth birthday. I loved that bike. It was a BMX and was fast.

My Delinquent Activities

We started smoking that year. We'd use the soda money our parents gave us and all chip in to buy a pack at this little burger and ice cream store. We'd lie and say they were for Mom, Dad, or Big Sis. We never got turned down. There was this big storm drain that ran under a street on the south part of town. We'd walk up into it, hang out, and smoke our cigarettes. No one was really inhaling yet but it didn't take long.

I vandalized my first building about then. It was a park's public bathroom. It started out as just playing around. We were kicking open the stall doors like we were cops kicking in doors. Then it just got out of hand. Before we were done, the sinks were kicked off the walls, the pipes were kicked loose, and the place flooded fast.

We never got caught for that, so we never really learned how wrong it was. This was the time in my life when I could have used an involved parent. I was pushing a lot of

176

boundaries but wasn't being caught for any of them. I just got into the habit of doing what I wanted and didn't have anyone telling me some of this was wrong.

By Halloween we went out egging houses. We stole gum from one friend's uncle's store. We would ride our bikes through the courthouse just for kicks. We'd make prank phone calls, throw stink bombs all over town, break pay phones, and throw snowballs at moving cars - some on city streets, others on the highway. We were so misbehaved that one of our friend's parents seriously considered not letting his son hang out with us anymore. I was never punished for this type of behavior, so I just continued to do it. I had no real restraints.

School at this small town wasn't as difficult as my old school, so I managed to stay above flunking. I still had the same attention problems. I would only do partial assignments and slop my way through spelling, word usage, punctuation, and other grammatical skills.

It didn't take long for the arguing to start at home. After a while, it became more open and more often. The day before Christmas Eve, we packed up while he was at work and moved back to Grandma's house. That was the end of stepdad number six.

My grades slipped when we went to school that spring, but at the end of the year I was passed anyway. I had failed the year before, and they didn't want to put my development at a disadvantage, so I was sent to the seventh grade that next fall.

Again, my behavior was unchecked, and I'd do things that I shouldn't have, like kick over mailboxes, throw rocks, ride my bike through the college fountain, and even climb up onto the roof of a business for kicks. To me, it was fun, not stupid! I know better now, but back then I simply did what I wanted.

By the fall, I had figured out how to empty candy out of the vending machines around town by using a coat hanger to "jimmy" the wires that held the candy in place. We stole sandwiches out of sandwich machines by opening the back panel and rotating the trays the food sat on. It was never a question of right or wrong. It was there! I wanted it! So I just took it!

We were living in a crappy apartment building. After we had worn out our welcome and were behind on the rent, we moved back to Grandma's house once again. However, before we moved back, my brother and I finally crossed a line and got busted.

There was a hotel up the highway from where we lived. A couple of buddies, my brother, and I went there to shoot pool. We were all smoking and setting our cigarettes down on the edge of the table to make our shots. A staff member of the hotel came up to us and, in a real snobby and condescending voice, informed us, "If any of you burn that table, you'll be paying for it."

We simply said, "Ok, we'll be careful" and out of earshot said, "F— you." One kid, not a close friend, quipped, "My dad's a doctor. He could probably buy this shitty hotel."

Every flick of ash was now pressed onto the felt top of the pool table and the cigarettes were put out on the floor. We decided it would no doubt prove our coolness to throw the plastic pool furniture into the pool. We decided to take a fire extinguisher and throw it out of a second floor window.

With that, we decided it was time to go. We were all pretty excited and thought that what we had just done was to take a stand. "They'll think twice about f—ing with us after this," we thought. But we had been recognized by a couple visiting the hotel and three of us were charged. The doctor's kid got off with a warning and he pointed the finger at us.

We were waiting to see what would happen when my brother, a friend involved in the hotel caper, and I vandalized a hiking trail. We pulled down signs, tore up older wooden steps, and destroyed two foot bridges. This time there was no "stand taken" because we just broke the stuff. We were stupid!

Our big mouths got us caught. We bragged about it to a kid in the neighborhood, and he told his parents. They called the cops. So add another charge to the first one. That summer, I was put on probation for a year, as was my brother. We were ordered to do community service and to pay a fine. We did our community service at a local activities center and the Salvation Army. It wasn't hard work, but it wasn't fun there. When we worked at the Salvation Army, we stole things.

My mother started seeing a guy that summer. They were together all of a week, and they were married. Enter stepdad number seven. He was pretty cool, easygoing, funny, and more like a friend than a stepdad. He liked to drink, though, and liked to punch stuff when he was drunk. He never hit any of us. He was small; my brother and I were fourteen and we were bigger than him. He sometimes let us get drunk with him. My brother was a loud, goofy drunk, doing stupid stuff like dunking his head in the toilet. Later on, we started smoking pot with him. He wasn't a very good role model and only fed our delinquent behavior. He would tell us stories about all the trouble he got into when he was a kid.

There wasn't much time that passed before the fighting started. Mom would say he had been drinking too much. We moved back to Grandma's house. Just before Christmas break, Mom left and divorced number seven. The previous school year we had failed again, and so when the fall came we started the seventh grade over. The school year was finally coming to an end. I had been passed, not on grades but on the best interest of my development.

My cousin was more like a sister to me than my own sister. My brother and I always looked at her as if she were a triplet. We did a lot of stuff together over the years. She was there when my dad beat my mother and me. We would all go out and get drunk, including my mother. My cousin, brother, and I would smoke weed together. My mother knew but didn't say much. She'd protest at times, but we would just do it anyway.

That summer would be my last summer of freedom, but before it ended I found myself in trouble again. A couple of days before school was out, there was a track and field competition between the homerooms. I thought it would be cool to take some tequila to this field day. You can't be cool unless people know about it. Well, when too many people know, someone is bound to tell. A teacher had heard of the contraband and came to investigate. When he took a sip, I told him that it was "Swiss-English tea," but he busted me.

I was sent to see my probation officer who was quite disappointed with me. Later that summer, I was given six months more probation, more community service, and forty-eight hours in detention. Every day that summer I went to my drug treatment center. They only dropped a urine test on me once, but I was clean so they believed I was doing good. However, I was smoking pot whenever I could get it and even gave some to two of the guys in the group home section of the treatment center.

I went to the forty-eight hour detention at the end of summer. It seemed longer. Basically, I sat in the cell most of the time. I came out to play volleyball, once to shower, and once to watch a movie. Mostly, I was just bored. When I came home, the stereo and TV were gone. We had gotten behind on payments. Mom had lost her job a month or so earlier and money was tight. We got a TV from Grandma, so we'd have something to watch.

Events Leading to the Murder

We started the eighth grade that fall and began hanging around a guy we had known most of our lives. We were cool with his younger brother, too. We would go over to his house and smoke pot. He introduced us to huffing gasoline to get high. It was very cheap and very effective. We used the gas can like a bong. We'd open the breather hole and suck air from the nozzle. The trip was fun. Sometimes, you hallucinate and see weird things. Later, I learned the "high" is your brain being slowly starved of oxygen. The gas coats your lungs and doesn't allow the effective transfer of oxygen or release of carbon dioxide.

As my eighth grade school year progressed, I spent more time smoking pot, getting drunk, and huffing gas. I got assigned to a G.E.D. class so I could just learn what I needed to get a diploma and drop out. A G.E.D. was my way out of day-long boredom. I wanted more freedom and started pushing my limits - staying out late, sneaking out, stuff like that. My mom would try to punish us, but we didn't see it as punishment.

One day my brother and I tried to doing something responsible. We called a family meeting and tried to discuss our issues. But we were pretty much laughed at. I snapped and threw something across the room. At that point, I just said, "F— it!" I was filled with anger and tried to walk it off, but Mom picked me up about five blocks away and took me home. So instead I brooded in my room.

It was harder and harder to just deal. My life wasn't bad, but I felt it was. To me at the time I felt misunderstood, not given enough freedom, and powerless to change the things that were wrong.

One Friday in early fall my pot-smoking, gasoline-huffing friend had planned a "camping" trip. It really had little to do with camping. There were no tents or camping equipment. My pot-smoking, gasoline-huffing friend drove. His brother and girlfriend, another boy and girl we knew, and my brother and I were picked up in his car. I told my mom we were going camping. I didn't ask! I just said it! She didn't say no. My brother grabbed a blanket, and I grabbed my pipe.

We drove down a dirt road to a concrete bridge. Some of them had been here before on other "camping trips." Later we drove into town and got pot, which we all chipped in for. On the ride back, we used my pipe to smoke our weed. After a few hours back at the camp, we all left when the high wore off. But not before three of us - our pot-smoking and gasoline-huffing friend, my brother, and I had a conversation about running away.

I didn't really put much stock into what was said. We were high, so I figured it was just bullshit. I was wrong! The following Sunday my pot-smoking, gasoline-huffing friend called my brother and said, "This is it! We're gone! Get your shit! Let's go!"

We filled up our backpacks, tossed them out the back door, and left out the front. We walked the eight or nine blocks to his house where he was ready with his bag, too. He grabbed a baseball bat out of the backyard, and we left. The plan was to find an easy victim and car jack him, or find a car that was away from any prying eyes and break the ignition with a screwdriver.

We ended up walking by a car with the keys in the ignition, so we simply piled in and drove away. The drive was exciting and fun. We had some of our cassette tapes, and we played the radio as loud as it would go. We tried to peel out with the tires, but the car was a town car and had no real power. About two o'clock in the morning and a hundred miles from home, we came to the realization that we had no money and no way to get any, so we decided to go home. Our pot-smoking, gasoline-huffing friend said he had a gun we could use to hold people up for money.

At home, we caught hell from mom. She had called my probation officer. We told her we were at a college party with some college chick we met. She demanded to know where and who we said we were with. We wouldn't tell and she finally gave up.

The following day was normal until our pot-smoking, gasoline-huffing friend said the words to me that were the beginning of the end of life as we knew it and would take the life of an innocent person: "I've got my gun back. We're leaving."

We found my brother and headed out. Across from the school was a guy my brother and pot-smoking, gasoline-huffing friend knew, but who I had never met. He gave us a ride to the pot-smoking, gasoline-huffing friend's house. He went into his house, got his rifle, and grabbed a small bag of clothes.

We asked the driver to give us a life to the car we had "stashed" at an abandoned concrete factory. We also asked if he would give us a ride until we found a new car if the car wasn't there, and he agreed.

We drove the same route we used two nights previously. We listened to the radio, talked nonsense, and just enjoyed the ride. The driver had taken his dad's SUV the night before and wouldn't let any of us drive. Our pot-smoking, gasoline-huffing friend was annoyed by this, but he let it go.

We talked about robbing gas stations or houses, or pulling cars over and jacking them. But every time we would find excuses, such as "it's too open," "that car is too noticeable," or "there is probably someone home." Stuff like that! I thought it was all talk, and we didn't really intend to do anything but keep driving. That would change!

I'm positive all the events leading up to the crime are real. The actual murder is a blur to me, and I'm not sure what really happened. You ask yourself: "Can a murderer be traumatized by the act of killing" The answer is yes!

I was fifteen. The most violent thing I had ever done was getting into a school yard fight that lasted two punches, only one of which connected. I felt guilty for that!

Our trip had taken us several hours from home. My pot-smoking, gasoline-huffing friend was getting impatient and eager to be rid of our driver. He thought that getting a car to continue on our own was priority number one. He had our driver back up into a field drive (a small short access to a field or pasture), and we sat and waited for cars to pass.

Earlier when the trip started, my pot-smoking, gasoline-huffing friend had asked us, "Who's good shot?" Proud of my skill, I quickly spoke up. He said, "Here's the gun, man," and handed me the .22 rifle. I didn't argue or dispute his assignment.

Like any good hunter or gunman I checked over my weapon. I found three bullets and an automatic bolt that wouldn't completely close. The gun was broken. My pot-smoking, gasoline-huffing friend and my brother took turns using a flathead screwdriver to poke around inside the gun. Finally, it slid close. Carefully, I slid a bullet into the barrel with my fingers. Uncertain of the gun's capability to actually fire, I put it out the window and above the roof. If it backfired, we wouldn't be hurt. The gun fired, but the action bolt was again stuck open. After using the screwdriver for an hour or so, my brother managed to get the bolt closed again. We knew the gun would fire but only once.

As we drove up to the field drive, we had been laughing and joking. While we were sitting in the field drive, our pot-smoking, gasoline-huffing friend changed seats with the driver. He was believed to be the better driver. The gun was passed to me in the passenger seat, and we waited. Several cars passed by. We decided that they were the wrong kind of car or had too many people inside. We selected a car and pulled out after it.

It took us a while to chase it down. We used a flashing light bar on the roof to pull over the car (the previous driver's father had been a mail deliverer and used this vehicle in delivering mail). When it stopped, I opened my car door and put the gun in the "V" of the door. My pot-smoking, gasoline-huffing friend got out and used a flashlight to shine in the woman's eyes. He told her he was a cop and to get out of the car.

At this point my adrenaline was very high. I was overwhelmed with a thousand different thoughts. I had tunnel vision. I remember my brother and the driver talking at me. I don't think I really ever heard them. It was just background noise. My pot-smoking, gasoline-huffing friend came back to the car and said, "She won't get out. Shoot the bitch."

This whole trip I had been telling myself it was all talk. I'd never have to do anything. At that moment, I wasn't torn. I didn't stop myself and say, "Hey, what are you doing?" It was just automatic. My friend said, "Shoot!" I turned and shot.

I walked up to the car, but the door was locked. I kicked out the driver's window. The last thing I clearly remember as my own memory is looking into her face. Her eyes were dazed, and she looked like she had been punched. I felt like I was frozen in that moment for an hour. At some point, I pulled out a pocket knife and stabbed her over thirty times. I was told later that my brother had come up to the car and tried to pull me away. I said to him, "She won't die. Please, God, why won't she die?"

My brother used the stock of the gun to push her away and to push me out of the window. He said, "Lady, just give us your purse." With the last of her strength, she managed to toss her purse to my brother. I remember my brother screaming at me, "We've got to go!"

I looked down at my hands, and they were covered in blood. I couldn't figure out how it got there. Then I saw the knife and freaked out. I wiped my hands over my shirts and threw the knife as far as I could. It was more of an attempt to get it out of my hand than to conceal the murder weapon. I took off my denim shirt and dropped it in the ditch.

I could only think, "Did I? Did I really?" I was asking myself a question but wasn't sure of what I was asking. It was like I was talking to myself, and there were two of me inside my head. One of me was saying, "Did you really do that?" And the other knew what I had done.

I don't remember getting back into the truck or talking to the others. I remember being pulled out of the truck and water poured over my hands to wash off the blood. The truck was over heating, and the person who was now driving instead of my pot-smoking, gasoline-huffing friend had pulled up to a farm house to get water for the radiator.

I woke up the next morning asleep in the back of the SUV. The seat was folded down. My brother and I had slept there. The driver and my pot-smoking, gasoline-huffing friend had slept in a motel room, purchased with the credit card number of the driver's grandmother. He had called her to get the number. The driver came down, got my brother and me, and took us up to the room. We all showered and sat around watching TV.

My pot-smoking, gasoline-huffing friend had called his mother, and she had called the police in that town. She told them that we were runaways. They came to the motel and brought us to the station while we waited for our parents to come and get us.

I wouldn't let myself think about the night before and kept acting like a goof, telling jokes and laughing at stuff that wasn't really funny. It was a defense mechanism because I was terrified to think about the night before.

Arrested, Convicted, and Sentenced

My mother made us turn ourselves in for jacking that town car the first time we ran away. The elderly couple who owned the car agreed to not press charges if we returned their keys and atlas, which we did. We also wrote apology letters.

I was overwhelmed with guilt and couldn't think of anything else all week. My probation officer was upset but seemed to understand, and he wanted to help us work out our problems. I believed then that my life would go back to normal and no one would ever know what I had done.

The Friday of that week I knew differently. The driver had confessed his participation to a friend, and it didn't take long for word to spread. That same day two cops came to our town, found our juvenile officer, and scheduled an interview for the next day with all four of us. We all showed up and professed our innocence, but under the weight of our guilt and the skill of the interrogators, we all admitted our guilt and signed confessions.

That was my last day of freedom. I was a month away from my sixteenth birthday. I was put in a detention center, but I was still telling myself it would all be okay. I could not have really done it! Surely this was a mistake and everything would work out. Later that day, a judge waived jurisdiction, and we were transported five hours from home to the county where the crime had taken place.

In January, I was waived to the adult court and transferred to an adult jail. This transition into incarceration wasn't completely unpleasant. My brother was still with me, so I wasn't alone. I still cried a lot then, but you can only cry so much before your tears dry up.

First there is denial, then bargaining. Not very religious, I turned to God. I begged for forgiveness and pleaded for freedom. Some of my guilt subsided, but not all of it. Freedom never came.

I've relived the events of my life a thousand times. I've relived my crime a million times. Why? What could I have done to stop it? What was wrong with me? How could I? Why? If only I had thought of the consequences.

We spent the next year and a half in county jail going through disposition, pre-trial motions, and preparation for our individual defenses. I never was a big reader in school, but having nothing but free time, I started reading novels and fell in love with reading. It was an escape from my reality, another world I could lose myself in. I am still quite a reader.

Eventually, our individual cases were separated, and we were all give separate trials. The driver turned states' evidence and got a deal. He still ended up with a hefty sentence. The rest of us went to trial, and we were found guilty one-by-one and sentenced. In the end, it took the jury in my case about two hours to come back with the verdict: Guilty on both counts of first-degree murder and first-degree robbery.

The three of us were given life sentences without the possibility of parole. I wasn't really scared because I knew I would lose, I was just going through the motions; emotionally, I detached as I often did when I was uncomfortable in a situation.

Two things stick in my mind about my trial that I probably will never forget. One is that although I tried not to look, I couldn't help but see the crime scene photos. I was horrified and never more ashamed of myself than at that moment. The second thing is that after the jury read its verdict and I was leaving the courtroom, the victim's father walked up to me very casually and said, "It's just too damn bad they don't have the death penalty." I remember thinking his eyes didn't even look human. He had so much hate, anger, and pain in his eyes. I never dreamed I could inspire such angst and misery.

Incarceration

It has been eight years since I was sent to prison. Prison has changed me. I've been through and done things I never thought I would go through. The word "prison" may bring to mind different things for different people, but for most, it's the movie version of what prison is supposed to be like. The reality of prison is much more complicated, though no less dramatic.

At seventeen, prison was many things for me. There is the fear; we've all seen the movies where the young kid comes into prison and is quickly fed upon by the predators. He's raped, beaten, or killed, sometimes all of the above. I have a very active imagination, so I could foresee every possible bad outcome, played out in vivid detail inside my head. You tell yourself, "I'll be strong. I'd do whatever it takes to survive," but the fear is still there.

Everything is so uncertain. You have no idea what to expect. It's a feeling of flux, and for a time, your life simply doesn't belong to you. It's like you were a caterpillar sealed away inside your cocoon. You're constantly changing. You have to learn to adapt to your new environment.

It's a proving ground. You're constantly being tested. "Will he, won't he? Is he, can he?"

The other inmates, as well as staff, feel you out to see if you're a snitch, a bitch, a gossip, or a "stand up" or "solid" guy. They want to know if you're strong and can take of yourself.

When we first pulled up to the prison, it was intimidating and looked like a castle. I had some problems early on about guys hitting on me. One guy really worked me, but I made a knife in my cell and stabbed him in the neck. I was really scared. He got the knife away from me, but I stuck my finger in his neck. Guards broke it up, but he nearly died. I got an attempted murder charge out of it, but everyone pretty well left me alone after that.

Do I deserve to be here? Probably! Regardless of my age, what I did was wrong. Regardless of my mental status at the time of the crime, what I did resulted in a spouse who lost his wife, four young kids growing up without a mother, and an innocent person losing her life. Do I feel guilty? Not as much as I used to. As the years pass and the more I go through, it's harder to feel sorry or guilty.

I don't like being in prison, but for the most part, I like the man I am today. There are, of course, things about myself I don't like, and they are directly related to my environment. Still, I see how members of my family and some of my closest friends turned out. They are strung out on drugs, and their lives are miserable. I know that could have been me. Had I not come to prison, my life could have ended up like that of most of the people I know: strung out and living a life of unhappiness and meaninglessness. I would rather be who I am than as the person I could have ended up. There is always the possibility that I could have avoided all of that and turned out okay. We'll never know though.

I still long for freedom but have accepted my fate. If I could change it, I would, but I don't dwell on freedom like some guys do. Life is full of surprises. Who knows? Fifteen years from now they might pass some law or vacate a number of sentences. I'll never give up hope or the dream of freedom, but I'm not going to obsess over it. I have my life, and I'll get as much out of it as I can. I'll leave you with one last insight. I heard somewhere the question "What is the meaning of life?" I had that question stuck in my head for several years and finally I came up with an acceptable answer, "The meaning of life is what life means to you."

CRITICAL THINKING QUESTIONS

1. Why do you think this twin killed the woman in the stopped car? What explains the viciousness of this attack (that he stabbed her over thirty times)?

2. What explanations of delinquency best explain his previous delinquent acts as well as the murder?

3. What do you think of the way he is processing and making sense of his life? Does his response seem to be typical?

4. If you were a member of the jury, would you have voted to give him a sentence of life imprisonment with no possibility of parole? If not, what sentence would you have given him?

22

Forgotten Children

Being born in a society that has every blessing known to mankind, it is very strange that so many of its precious children are denied the basic nourishments that would truly enrich the country, as well as the lives of others.

Children like myself who were, and are, in homes of abuse find it very hard to deal with life. We are left to discover what it means to get proper rest, what it means to eat a nourishing meal, what it means to respect the rights and property of others, what it means to love, what it means to hate, what is right and wrong, and what it means to have God in our lives.

How can the undeveloped mind of a child take on all the responsibilities of an adult, when all the wonderment of childhood has been erased by the coldness of life?

At a young age, my eyes witnessed my father taking his failures, disappointments, and frustrations out on the body of my mother. That made me feel that I was unable to protect someone that I loved.

Later in my life, the effect of watching this abuse made me attack anyone that I felt was abusing someone I believed that I loved. Be it physically, mentally, or spiritually, I would attack because these were my only avenues of defending those I felt were being abused.

I was taught by society that I was one of the unworthy children of its blessings because of my skin color. I had been raised by society to be a child of destruction, and so the respect that I should have had for another's rights, person, or property became unimportant to me. What had been instilled in an undeveloped mind, hurting soul, and unloved heart was that what I wanted or needed I could attain by force or brutality.

Home was not a place of warmth, love, concern, or respect, and so I found all those things in the environment of all those, like myself, who had been denied the same as I have been. Now I was in with a group of individuals who had no understanding or respect for life, trying to survive the coldness of a society that paid no attention to its children or cared about anyone other than those who they professed to love.

The street life teaches that if you are willing to do whatever it takes to make sure that those of your group, as well as yourself, are taken care of, then you have the strength and right to guide the group. Which in many ways means you can instill your own concepts, beliefs, and rules into those who follow you.

For a child who has never been given any attention, it is a great accomplishment to now have others to listen to your directions, as well as your vision of life, but it is also dangerous to those following, as well as to society. Because now an undeveloped mind, hurting heart, and unforgiving soul sits in a position of power and becomes someone who rules with an iron fist.

It is said that you should be careful with what you create because it may come back to haunt you or bless you. But the ingredients mixed into what is created will determine whether it haunts or blesses us.

I began breaking into buildings around my neighborhood and even into a few homes of those who were in the same condition as I was. I even stole from my own home and sold the items to drug dealers for money or other people who were out for a good deal.

Eventually it led to my first encounter with law enforcement officials at the age of eleven. I had broken into the neighborhood store, and those involved with me informed the officers after they were caught that I was the leader.

I was taken to jail and remained there until I was tried and sentenced to one year in training school. Once I was taken to the training school, I began to learn a lot about criminal activities. It was a harsh experience of slave labor, such as picking beans, corn, and peanuts. We killed pigs and cows, and lived in a dorm with forty other inmates. This took away the privacy that I had taken for granted when I was out in society.

The thing about being incarcerated is the fact that someone else has control over your actions and uses force as the main tool to get you to do what they order. At that time, the law allowed those who govern to beat inmates as a first option of punishment. So, I received many beatings for refusing to obey instructions given to me that I was felt were disrespectful.

These beatings only made me hate society even more, because it was society that I blamed for my condition at the time. But also unconsciously I began to hate my mother because of her lack of attention to me. I did not realize that at the time, society also had my mother under its oppressive foot. She was denied decent wages so that she could not properly provide for a family of nine children.

All of my concerns for family disappeared as I became more comfortable in the "penal system," as they call it. The penal system became my family in the sense that all those in the environment, in one way or another, had the same destructive mentality. It is already known that those who are strong will lead mostly by the negative. The positive really never has a chance to assert itself. What we have to do is to put aside our human traits; what is normal on the outside becomes abnormal on the inside.

It is not the institution that has the greatest effect on the person; it is the environment of individuals that will determine the real outcome on an attitude change. Those people like myself, who are placed in these environments, are forced to adapt to them for the sole purpose of human survival.

I, like so many others, became cruel in order to keep cruelty from being forced upon me by those who were suffering the same as I was in the same situation of oppression. I became unforgiving, so that no one could get away with any disrespect or mistreatment, as I saw it to be. When those concepts are the foundation of a person's character, they just don't go away once that person is released into society.

I did a total of six to seven years in and out of training school for crimes like breaking and entering, robbery, assault, and stealing. In those years I was one of the individuals who controlled my surroundings by force, and once I was released I carried that same mentality back into society.

It was not long before I graduated from training school to prison as an adult. I was sentenced first for five years for assault with the intent to do great bodily harm and sent to a minimum-security institution. Within nine months, because of an assault on another inmate, I was sent behind the walls of the state's maximum-security prison.

In the main prison environment, it is the toughest of the tough that rules, and the weak are open prey for all. It was a quite different lifestyle because everyone has some type of weapon. With the time I had, I could have been out in two years, but I got another five. So the five was now ten.

It is very strange how it is determined that someone is strong by how many they stab, rape, beat down, trick, or abuse. But in an environment that has no vision or direction, all that is left is anger, failure, disappointment, and frustration, which is what I saw my father use to abuse my mother.

It was not long before I was once again comfortable in the prison lifestyle. I began to do as I had done in my early years. I ruled with an iron fist and unforgiving soul. It was not long before I became known throughout the prison as someone who would not allow anyone to disrespect me or anyone else in my group. But like all of prison's ordeals, one must set many examples before he is truly respected and feared. So I went about setting the examples that kept me in the solitary unit more than I was in the population. I was denied honor time and good time that is given to those who conduct themselves according to the rules. So now, instead of just doing four years, ten months, and eight days on a ten-year sentence, I was doing a straight ten years.

With thirty-two days before being released, I was charged with two counts of murder, tried, convicted, and sentenced to two life death sentences. Since that time, some twenty-six years have passed. Here I sit in prison seeking to overcome the need for attention and seeking to overcome the deprivations of my childhood.

CRITICAL THINKING QUESTIONS

1. How does this inmate explain why he became a violent person?
2. What does he mean that all "the wonderment of childhood has been erased by the coldness of life"?
3. According to this inmate, how does one become a leader of others?
4. What effects did the juvenile system, especially institutions, have on this individual?
5. He blames a lot of his problems on environment. Do you agree, or has he overstated the case?

23

A Small-Town Boy

I grew up in a very small town, in one of the Great Lakes states, with a population of maybe 700. I was the youngest of three children. I had a brother who was one year older and a sister who was five years older. My sister had a different father, whom she never met, from my mother's first marriage. My mother never spoke of him, even in later years. My sister always considered my father to be her real father.

Our family was on the lower end of the socioeconomic scale. My mother was only a high school graduate with no skills other than an aptitude for numbers, which she used in bookkeeping jobs to support us. My father came down with multiple sclerosis when I was two or three years old. He was confined to his wheelchair until I was about six or seven years old, then his affliction gradually progressed and he was hospitalized permanently. He had lost all use of his limbs and he could not feed himself or take care of himself in any way. His speech was so slurred it was a real struggle for him to even speak. I was very sad when our mother would take us to visit him, because we had to see him in this condition. I felt so sorry for him and my mother. I remember how courageous I thought he was when he would tell my mother that she was still young and should go out and find another man. My mother did start seeing a man who eventually became my stepfather. My father died when I was fifteen years old. He was 46 years old when he died, and my mother was only 40. I attended his funeral, and it was my first experience dealing with the death of anyone. It left me feeling empty and cheated.

The only real memories I have of spending any time with my father was in his hospital room. I have no real memories of him being at home with us. All I have is a few photos of him in his wheelchair with us kids and him; everyone was happy and had big smiles.

My mother would leave me with my aunt and uncle when she would go visit my dad or wherever else she would go. They lived outside of town in the country. They had four boys and three girls. The girls were closer to my age and were tomboys, so we often played together. The boys were much older than me, by at least ten years. They were a loving family. I liked staying with them because there were a lot of things to do when we played outside. In the winter we would ice-skate on a little pond by their house. In the summer we would go hiking, play football or catch, climb trees, and all of the types of recreation kids like to do.

We were a poor family so we would get hand-me-down clothes, probably from Goodwill or other families. We never minded because getting used clothing was just like getting something new for us. Sometimes we could afford a few new clothes for the start of a new school year or at Christmas. My mother even went on A.D.C. for a while, to help make ends meet when she was only working at her part-time bookkeeping job. I don't think she even had a car for everyday use. My mother married my stepfather a few years before my dad died. He was from a neighboring town and had two kids from a prior marriage who lived with their mother. He was a salesman for a chemical company.

I was probably about six or seven years old when I began shoplifting candy from the local grocery store where my mother had a running account with the store's owner. My brother and I would stay in there after swimming at the local swimming creek and charge for pop and other goodies. This was the time when I started to pocket gum and candy. I started smoking probably at around nine or ten years old. I would sneak butts from my mother's and my aunt's ashtray. Eventually I started taking whole cigarettes from their packs, and later stealing whole packs from grocery stores. I would steal from any store or gas station, sometimes on my own, but usually I would do this with my best friend when we were together. Sometimes he would get the attention of whoever was watching the store or business while I would go to the display cabinet and slide the door open to get the cigarettes. We would only take a pack or two at a time when we stole them, but usually just one pack. We would also play with pinball machines and put our feet under the front legs to get the ball caught in a slot to rack up extra points to win free games.

We had moved to Chicago when I was about eleven or twelve years old to live with my grandmother. My sister had gotten married at eighteen. I was still smoking and started stealing waitresses' tips off of tables in a restaurant. I did this at least six or eight times. When I was ten years old I started stealing money from an aunt that was living with us. She was a waitress and kept a tip jar in my mom's bedroom. I stole from her jar at least four or five times, taking maybe three or four dollars each time. Once when I was about ten I went into cahoots with a couple other kids and stole a ring. The police took me down and questioned me about it. I think I denied it. When I was about ten years old the school principal's son and I started a grass fire, and we got caught. My mother punished me by strapping me with the branch off of a weeping willow tree that was in our front yard. This was the only real physical discipline or punishment I ever remember receiving, except for a few spankings.

I got caught stealing some money out of my grandmother's purse at thirteen. I didn't want to face my mother after this, so I ran away along with a couple of neighbor kids. We took a train 25 miles away, where the police caught us at the train station. I wasn't punished at all for this.

We moved to Milwaukee when I was fifteen years old. I was still smoking and started drinking a little beer on weekends and during summer evenings with high school friends. I started shoplifting clothes from various department stores. I was jealous of some of the other kids' clothes, clothes which I did not have and could not afford to buy. I only got caught one time and that was for stealing a bracelet. I was given a scare speech, after a ride in the police car, and a threat to call my parents.

When I got my first job, I was thirteen. It was at an A&W in my hometown one summer, when I returned to visit. I was stealing the waitresses' tips, a little here and there, and finally I got caught. When asked about it by the owner, I denied it. I don't know why I didn't have any problem lying when confronted about these types of things.

I did start working part-time at sixteen so I could have my own money. I was washing dishes and working on a yard crew, cutting grass and laying sod.

One night when I was sixteen or seventeen years old, I was with this guy who was a year older than me. We were on his motorcycle and went to a home secluded in the country. To my surprise, he broke into this home. I went in with him and he stole some items. I had never done anything this brazen before. This is the same fellow who got me stoned on marijuana; I about freaked out and became very paranoid.

When I was seventeen years old, I moved to Omaha with my mother and stepfather. I was still stealing clothes and record albums in a big shopping mall. Sometimes I would return the clothes for a cash refund. While still living in Milwaukee, we would go into people's garages late at night to steal beer. We would also go to bars to drink beer at sixteen or seventeen, and to summer beer tents in various small towns at summer picnics. Sometimes we would just steal liquor from our parents' liquor cabinets and put water back in the bottles. Once in a great while I would steal a dollar from my mother's purse.

I believe a lot of my juvenile delinquency was the result of not having a father to discipline me or to provide a positive role model. I had too much time on my hands when there wasn't an adult around to provide the necessary discipline. I believe I was also rebelling due to not having a father and not having money to buy nice things. My time spent with my uncle and older male cousins wasn't enough to provide that necessary discipline. My mother would scold and threaten me with whippings if I got way out of line, but I knew she would usually cave in and not do anything. I think I may have also rebelled since she was seeing my stepfather while our real father was still alive, even if he did give his blessing to her seeing someone else. I felt cheated that I didn't have a real--healthy--father who could spend time with me. I did not have someone to take me fishing, camping, and swimming, or play baseball with, like other kids do. I think I was angry that he had MS and had to suffer and struggle to even speak; it just wasn't fair. His death and seeing him in a casket just left me feeling abandoned and hollow.

I never really accepted my stepfather. I think I resented him, and sometimes I think this resentment would surface towards my mother, never surfacing in any verbal outburst, but just underlying feelings of anger. It usually happened when she would go on dates with my stepfather and they'd stay out late. His wife would call our house occasionally and ask if he was there and give my sister a hard time, which would really upset her. One night I grabbed the phone when she called, because my sister was crying. I cussed this woman out and told her that we would kill her if she didn't leave us alone. I was only ten or eleven years old when that happened. I love my sister, brother, and mother very much. I would never let anything bad happen to them. I think this woman would threaten our mother during some of these calls. When I was charged with my present crime 20 years ago, I was diagnosed as suffering from hysteria. I'm now wondering if these earlier experiences with the phone calls, which caused my sister to experience hysteria, may have also caused my hysteria. I was arrested when I was seventeen years old for theft. I was with a kid who put car tape players in a shopping cart and tried to walk out of the store without paying for them. We were both taken to jail. My mother came down and got me out, but she was very upset. I don't think I was ever charged for that crime.

In 1968 when I graduated from high school, I was eighteen years old. Another kid and I smoked some grass or drank some beers and decided to try to break into a house. We were not even in the house when a neighbor came out and held a gun on us until the police came. I was placed on probation for attempted residence burglary. It was about this time I started experimenting with more marijuana and drinking. Mostly I was just smoking grass, but eventually I tried LSD. I was out on my own then as my parents had moved to Michigan. I stayed in Omaha since I had a girlfriend and a job, and my own apartment. I started selling a little marijuana, some hashish, and once in a while some LSD. In 1970 I sold some hash and two hits of LSD to an undercover cop. They tried to turn me into a rat, but I just could not bring myself to actually set someone up. I was going to put some drugs into an old house that I had in the ghetto. I thought I could tell the cops there were drugs there, so that I would not go to prison. Before I could follow through on this, I had been arrested again. I was at a house where the police found some marijuana. When I went for sentencing on the sales charge, I tried to change my guilty plea by claiming I had been entrapped. I said that I had already spoken with another attorney and wanted to go to trial, but the judge wouldn't go for it. He sentenced me to three to five years in the reformatory. I guess the cops were pissed because I didn't fulfill my agreement and I gave them the runaround. Nine months later my conviction was overturned because the judge hadn't allowed me to withdraw my earlier plea, and there was no factual basis for my guilty plea. That made me very happy.

Prior to being arrested in 1970, I had worked at a head shop for almost two years. The shop sold everything from rolling papers to bell-bottomed jeans. I was selling a little pot and hash out of the shop and began to pocket some cash from the legitimate sales. I also began taking posters and other items without paying for them. Again, I had no guilty conscience for doing this. I knew it was wrong, but I didn't really care about anyone except myself. The man I worked for even let me live at his apartment. I practically ran his business when he was out of town on buying trips. He was very kind and we remained friends over the years. He even visited me in prison in 1983. I'm not proud of a lot of my actions now that I have had time to reflect.

I also realize that I committed fraud several times. I bought traveler's checks and claimed they were lost. I got a refund by having my buddy cash the checks before they were on the hot sheet. Back then all the check-casher needed was a little identification and a person who could forge your signature.

Over the years, between the ages of 18 and 31, I used several different drugs. My big downfall was taking tranquilizers with alcohol at the same time. One evening I made a terrible decision while under the influence of this drug combination. It resulted in the death of a girlfriend and cost me the rest of my life in prison. I truly regret my actions. I wasn't always stealing, committing fraud, or dealing drugs. I held down a full-time job from 1975 until 1980, which was eight months prior to my current incarceration. I've had many jobs that required responsibility. I never had any violence on my record prior to the current offense I'm doing a life sentence for. I know that certain drugs mixed with alcohol will cause you to make bad choices you would not make otherwise. Anyone who has kids needs to talk to them very seriously, and tell them about how harmful the effects of drugs and alcohol really are. Peace.

CRITICAL THINKING QUESTIONS

1. How did his father's condition affect what happened to this young man?
2. Why was stealing such an important part of his life?
3. How did his mother affect what took place in his life?
4. Is it surprising that drugs became such an important part of his life?

24

My Father Was an Alcoholic

My family has always been dysfunctional. I can't remember a time when we really got along. My father is an alcoholic. As long as I can remember, he has been a heavy drinker.

At three years old, I fell off a slide while at a playground, and I fell on my head. This incident was the start of a very confusing childhood for me.

At five years old, I lit my father's bed on fire while he was asleep on it, and then I crawled under the bed because I was so scared of my father. I knew what he would do and I'd rather face the fire than my father. My father dragged me out from underneath the burning bed, even though I was trying to hold on to the burning bed leg because I was so afraid of my father. He pulled me out, and I ran and hid, but he did not beat me this time.

Again at five years old, I stabbed my sister in the eye with a scissors. I am not sure why I did this to my sister. Still at five years old, my father hit me in the eye with a light bulb. He was drunk and he took out his anger out on me because he was arguing with my mother. He always called me names like mother f— and b—.

Also, at five years old, I stood up on a chair and unlocked our door. I went to a store 200 feet away from the house, and stole a six-pack of Pepsi Cola. I learned this behavior from my brother. Finally, I was five years old when we moved from one bad neighborhood to another. We moved after my dog Pete got hit by a car. I was always an animal lover when I was young, and still am to this day.

When we moved, my father's drinking got worse. I was always getting beaten for anything I did. When my father chased my brother and me into the closet, my brother used to hold me in front of him, and I used to get his beatings as well as mine. My father used his fists and his feet to discipline us, and at that time there was no laws prohibiting this beating. My dad would also take my bike and lock it in the shed so I could not ride it. He would also take my shoes to work with him, so I could not go outside and play.

The only thing that my father ever did with me was to take me fishing two times. He also took me to the fights (boxing) three times at the public auditorium. He never took me to baseball games or anything else that little boys would like to do. Father would make me go to the bar with him, and I could not stay at home with my mother because she couldn't control me. My mom split my head open twice because I would not listen to her. She didn't do it on purpose because she would throw things at me and most of them would not hit me.

My father even hit me with a rolling pin. He didn't know how to show love in any way. He use to treat my two sisters, my brother, and myself very mean by saying, "I wish you were never born, and all you kids do is cost me money."

On my confirmation--I went to Catholic school--my father asked me what I wanted, and I said, "Ham." So the next day my father brought a ham from the store that he never went to before. Then he cooked it until it was done. We sat down to eat with my aunt and uncle and their son. The ham was salty, real salty, and he blamed me for it. Then he started calling me a little p— b—s. Then he said that I just cost him twenty dollars for a ham that was all salt. My aunt and uncle told my dad that it wasn't my fault and to stop yelling at me. I thought I had done something wrong so I got up and hid.

I remember thinking that night that I wished I were dead. I also wished that my father were dead. I began to cuss God out for not helping me. I didn't do anything wrong, but I still I got blamed for something that I had no control over. I was only about nine or ten years old when this incident took place.

My mother also blamed me for her mother's death. She said that I kept her from going to see her dying mother. I also got yelled at for that. I had no control over my mother visiting her mother. My grandmother only lived about two miles away. This hurt because I don't believe I should have been blamed for it.

Processing through the System

At about age eleven, I started getting into trouble for being uncontrollable at home. I never listened to my mother and father. I think I was hyperactive. As the youngest of four children, I was the worst one of them. I started going to detention homes for youths, and I'd get out and be bad again.

The first time that I was locked up was in Pennsylvania George Junior Republic (PJR). That was for incorrigibility. I was locked up in this facility for eleven months. Then I went to live my cousin in Cleveland Heights. This did not last very long because I committed my first crime. This crime was purse snatching. I did not need the money because I was getting a ten-dollar allowance. I just did it. I also skipped school and snatched other purses. Then, I would get caught and be sent back to PJR. While at PJR, I learned about drugs and other mischievous behaviors. I didn't like it there; I didn't like being away from home, and I tried to escape twice.

I was fourteen years old when a schoolteacher at the Catholic school--there was a shortage of nuns--started playing around with me, kissing me. This was a woman twice my age; I felt like I was on cloud nine. Then she decided she liked another younger student, so I throw an egg at her that did not even hit her directly. I was sent away because of this incident to Boys Industrial School (BIS). I spent thirteen months there. When they realized that they could not control me, they sent me to TICO (Training Institution, Central Ohio).

At TICO, the staff had trouble controlling me, and I tried to escape three times. Three days before my eighteenth birthday, I was released from TICO. When I was at TICO, I got into a lot of fights. At TICO, I met a Mr. Bartollas who was trying to help me. He saw things in me that no one else did. He worked with me for about a year. He couldn't really figure me out. But he knew I had a lot of issues, including my mental health issues. He was the only one that really did try to help me!

Back to the egg and schoolteacher incident. I was sent to BIS with no trial, no nothing at all. They just locked me up, and this was the start of my life in crime. At age fourteen, I smoked grass, and dreamed about a life of drugs and crime. At age sixteen, I escaped from TICO, and that was when I got into hard drugs like heroin. When I was released from TICO, all I wanted to do is drink and do drugs. This was a life in the fast lane.

I did not see much love growing up. For what little love I did receive from my mother, my father and mother destroyed it by beating me. My father never received love from his mother or father. My father is treating me as his parents treated him. Still, when I was growing up, I always tried to avoid trouble but trouble always seemed to follow me. I tried to avoid fights, because I was good with my hands. I was beat on a lot when I was younger by my peers, which made me stronger. I would always say, "Wait until I am

201

bigger than *you; you* won't want to pick on me then." When I got older this became a reality.

On to Adult Crime

Then at eighteen, I was sent to Mansfield as an adult. I did 38 months, and got out and could not find a good job that paid over $1.50 an hour. So I turned to crime and drugs again because that was the thing to do. I moved to Akron, Ohio with my girlfriend and got into some trouble there.

I caught a murder case there and was sentenced to prison for the remainder of my natural life. It's sad, because I should have received a manslaughter charge that is only 7 to 25 years. This is just another injustice to me from the court system.

While in prison I had to fight, stab, and defend myself. I have been jumped several times and stabbed by inmates and beaten by prison guards at least five times. I was a young man thrown in with wolves.

I have seen men get killed, raped, beaten, and this was just in the first month I was there. The first month in prison, there were 27 stabbings and one person killed. I saw the person that got killed. I was only thirty feet away. This was a shock to me because I had only ever seen four people that had been killed in my life.

I remember in second grade I stopped a little boy from stabbing a little girl with his pocketknife. The nun was very proud of me. She even called my parents and told them I did a good thing. But when the boy's parents came to my house and said I hit their son, I got a beating. This one was a pretty big beating. I could not figure out why I was getting punished for doing something good. So no matter what I did--it seemed like good or bad--I got a beating for it.

So, now I am in prison and have been in prison for a long time. Prison has hardened me, and dehumanized me. In October 1997, I killed my cellmate that I knew for only four days. Why did I kill him? Well, the real reason why will go to the grave with me. I was sentenced to die for killing my cellmate. I sit here in Ohio on death row waiting to be executed.

Why has my life turned out the way it has? What is so sad is that down deep I am a kind, gentle, and loving person. I love animals, all of them. I love my mother and father with all my heart. When I was younger I hated them for the beatings that I received. But I have forgiven them.

I have come to the realization that the beatings were only a small part of my childhood. My abusive background certainly influenced my life of crime, but there is more to it than that. My mental disability has no doubt influenced my life of crime. Or it may be that the fall I took when I was three years old affected my brain functioning. Then, there were all those drugs I took. I guess I will never know what really went wrong inside of me. What I do know is that I am now the living dead.

Postscript—Clemens Bartollas

As a Ph.D. student at the Ohio State University, I worked full time as a social worker and then wing director at TICO. This young man was placed on my wing, and I took a special interest in him. We ran together a few times and had several conversations in my office. We gave him an early release because we did not feel that he belonged in this maximum-security training school for hard-core delinquents. I remember feeling uncomfortable about his future when he was released.

In 1998, I was hired as an expert witness for this person who was accused of committing a prison homicide. After nearly thirty years, we met again. It is very sad to me how his life has turned out.

CRITICAL THINKING QUESTIONS

1. If you were the wing director of TICO when this young man was there, what would you have said to him?
2. What explanation of delinquency best explains why he became a delinquent and went on to adult crime?
3. With his early background, do you believe that the state should have given him a death sentence for prison homicide?
4. If you knew the individual, as the author does, what would you say to him now? Write a letter to him and encourage him when he is really discouraged.

25

Selling Drugs Was My Downfall

This is my life. In the beginning we are all the same. The only difference is the elements that help to mold us--whether it is the environment, your heredity, or the willingness of the self to propel you to a limited or unlimited destiny.

I remember being in kindergarten at Oakton in Evanston, Illinois. Evanston is a nice suburb of Chicago. One day while playing on the slides and swings at school, a kid was above me with a brick in his hand. It was honest, I suppose, but as soon as I darted from the shelter of the swing, the brick smashed right onto my head. I lived only one block from school, so I ran home to my mother who was home with my baby sister. Instead of going to the teacher, my mother took me to St. Francis Hospital so I could get stitches, which I badly needed. This situation did not excite me, but it worried my mother. Two days after the brick incident, I punched the kid who dropped the brick on my head. This whole situation confused me because before the brick was dropped, the other boy and I were friends. Since that incident I retaliated and started acting "tough." This allowed me to give and get the respect I needed. It's weird how a dysfunctional character treats you decent when you treat them with no respect and vice versa.

I was young and was not prejudiced or biased in any way. I was blessed to be in a town that is diverse. I played with white kids as if they were my real brothers and sisters. I played with Amy and John most of my childhood. We three were inseparable from sun-up to sun-down. John was so clever at the age of eight. We would rob our piggy banks for candy or ice cream. These are just small things kids did. Life at that age was so simple and natural.

A year went past, and we moved to the South Side of Chicago. It looked like a nice neighborhood. Well, at least it was clean. The only problem I saw was there were some pretty bad hoodlums that hung out on the street corners. I remember having several of my neighbors in our backyard. One guy was my age, and his brother and two sisters were coaxing him to beat me in wrestling. I was naive, I just wanted to have fun, but the guy's siblings had a hidden agenda. I could hear them tell him to "smash" me, and make me pay. I was able to be stronger and faster than him. This was my welcome to Chicago.

Every day on my way to school there were these three guys, who were older, always standing in front of the candy store to steal kids' candy or lunch money. They got me one day. I couldn't fathom trying to fight one of these bullies, let alone all three. I didn't have a fighting bone in my body, and it was very hard on my psyche. I got up enough nerve on the third day to hit the smallest of the three; this actually worked. I singled him out and he backed down. It was a relief, because my mother was in seeing distance of the store, and she watched my every move. I was rewarded for that act of "bravery." I had new friends in the hood; girls would smile and giggle whenever I was around. I liked the attention that I received from them. That wasn't the end of my problem with bullies, because there were always bullies around. It was a matter of how good I could maneuver around them.

A friend of mine had a big yard, and one of the kids' favorite sports was tackle football. I was always good at football and also had good sportsmanship. Well, this other guy didn't, and he would try to scare me into not coming on his side. I had to stand up to him, besides we were the same size, and he did not have any football skills. So I decided to by him. I was fed up with his flaring up at me. He got in my face, and I pushed him with no response. Once again I won.

Now, as for school, I went to St. Bronislava Catholic School on 87th and Colfax from first grade to eighth grade. I was a class clown. When the nuns needed to discipline me, I was either put in the corner or a nun would pop me with a ruler on the hand. We were isolated from public school kids. We wore uniforms.

I was pretty intelligent, but it was not "cool" to be smart, so I stopped studying. My parents--who I adore more now than ever before--kept a belt on me to get my grades up, and I would for a while. Peer pressure was too strong for me then.

During my stay in Chicago, I got a glimpse of the gang activity, which claimed the neighborhoods. Whether you vocally accepted a gang or not, you had to stick together in order to survive the other gangs. The gang didn't necessarily start with violence, but if the threat was there, you were protected from being viciously jumped.

I came in contact with the Vice Lords in two ways. One way was through my cousin. The second way was that in our neighborhood a man in his forties would drive us all around in the back of his truck. He was a good man. He would even pick us up from school and buy us beer and wine. The whole hood was in the man's favor. We did not know until later that he was a Vice Lord leader. Now that I think back to it, he had us under his wing.

I began to steal candy or baseball cards with my friends. At this time I was about twelve years old. During this time, I believe gangs were not a huge issue for me because I had a paper route and my parents would send me to camp every summer. I hated camp at the beginning, but by the end I was crying because I did not want to leave. I always stayed busy.

When I reached eighth grade, our school couldn't financially support itself so it closed during the second semester. Our family moved back to Evanston this time for good. My first day at this school was fun. All the kids accepted me, and I had fun getting to know them. On my way home from school, I saw a guy running for his life from ferocious boys who were Vice Lords, so again I moved to a neighborhood where they had a stronghold.

It was natural for me to steal bikes. I seemed cut out for it. Even though I had two hard-working parents, it was easier for me to steal bikes and use their parts or trade them with friends. Don't get me wrong, I did the normal things, also, like shovel snow or rake leaves, but I just didn't do it enough. My best friend was already stealing dirt bikes and motorcycles at the age of fifteen.

We also loved video games, especially at the arcade. We were so good at finding ways to play the games free, like slamming pennies into Pac-Man or just plain breaking the lock and stealing the quarters out of it. Sometimes we would go to the arcade instead of school. My best friend wasn't in a "mainstream" school, so when we did go to school, we wouldn't see each other all day. The class he was attending was mainly for challenging kids with delinquent behaviors. This school seemed cool to me, but my parents would have never allowed it. At this early age I felt trapped between two worlds. One I knew was geared to success and the other one was doomed to failure. It was this second world that young black boys encountered.

At the age of sixteen, I was fully aware of my sexuality and I liked being around girls. Kissing was the thing for us guys in the 1980s. I still liked hanging with the fellas and finding something dangerous to get into. Like in the wintertime, we would throw snowballs at people--mostly men--to get them to chase us. I remember one particular time when a snow removal truck was dumping excess snow onto a bank. It was, like, seven of us, but five of them were three or four years older than me. One of the dudes hit the driver so hard he came out of his truck like a raving lunatic. We ran, but this guy wasn't all that old, maybe thirty-something. He caught me and pushed me hard into the snow. I am very lucky that that is all he did. Even with this happening, I still had not learned my lesson.

My buddies and I started to make it a ritual on the weekends to get drunk. We could get liquor from the local bootleg. With forty ounces of malt liquor and a pint of wine, I would be a laughing fool. With this new elixir, I was Don Juan or the coolest guy on the block. When I overdid it, I would get sick and vomit, but I only did this when I was trying to outdo one of my peers. Other times I would fight; often with alcohol, I would become a warrior.

Back then all you had to worry about was a knife or a baseball bat. Kids today have to worry about guns. I have so many friends from the past who have been gunned down in the name of "honor." It's terrible to see this happen, and to wonder about all the kids in prison for using alcohol and drugs. They are going through the same thing as a Vietnam veteran, or maybe even worse, because society has no clue, nor do they want to get involved. Some might say it's designed that way. As for me, I still have hope for the younger generation.

Growing up in the hood has its ups and downs. The pros are that everyone sticks together, and will lend a helping hand on "certain" aspects. There is a bond. The downside is if they can't relate to you, or even find that you have more than they do, well, its time you better move on or you can get hurt. They can treat you downright miserable.

My last year of high school I was so lost. I was still in school, but barely. I missed so many English classes the teacher didn't even really know my name. Somehow, I managed to get good grades. I would study and then go get drunk. My dad bought me a nice gold watch for graduation. I flashed the watch off while I walked across the stage for graduation. I wonder how my Pops had the patience for me.

A year later I joined the U.S. Army Reserve. Basic training was a gruesome situation, but I made it through it. I knew I had to get away from the hood. What astonished me was there were guys there who felt like I did. Their environment also consumed these *guys.* During our Advance Initial Training, we were allotted a weekend pass. All I can remember is getting drunk.

Coming home was great, even though I was only gone for three months. I noticed nothing had changed since my departure. I fell right back into the social structure of the hood, but this time it was worse. I met a girl who was a cocaine seller. She was adventurous and exciting. We would go to all the concerts we wanted to and go to go-cart places. The bad part was I started selling drugs with her. We would be in a crack house with the most hideous people you could ever imagine. I started out snorting "coke" recreationally. Then, as time progressed, I started smoking it. I tried my best to conceal my addiction from my parents, but there was no chance of it. As I look back, I see how I became quieter and more withdrawn while on coke. My daily activities were cut short because of my nightly drug use. I felt like a vampire.

During this time I was doing things I never thought I would ever be doing, like stealing cars and sleeping with women for money. One day I had enough willpower to escape, and I came to Des Moines, letting no one know where I had gone. I called my mom to let her know my whereabouts. She was worried, but I explained I was okay. I was in a town I didn't know, and people were strangers to me.

I was so stupid that I went back to Evanston and brought some cocaine to sell in Des Moines. The mark-up value was high and profitable. I had new associates now, but the same concept--ghetto life. I was stuck again with this crowd; the only difference is I didn't use cocaine.

I drank like a fish at this time and smoked more marijuana. In my conscience I tried to fool myself that I was better off not using, but it is okay to carry a gun and sell coke. Before I knew it, everyone in the slum world knew of me, and at that time I felt like a big man. I thought of myself as a good Samaritan because if I saw a pretty woman with a baby I would buy her and her child some diapers, milk, or food. It was my way of giving back at least a fraction of what I was taking from the hood.

It was near October when I met some guys from Kansas City who wanted to sell. So I helped one of them get on his feet. Every now and then I would front him some money, and he would pay me back later. On April 18, 1990, I was waiting for my *guy* to show up, but something felt funny this time. This time he came with two of his buddies. I also observed how he was talking so brazen to me when all I did was work with him. Next thing came out of his month was "You better hope I don't rob your ass." Right there I knew I had to stop all communication and get them out of my apartment. It was three-against-one odds. I had to pick my battle if I was going to win. So they left thinking they won. I knew they had guns because they stayed out of arms' reach of me, except for the one who owed me money.

Later that night I saw the thugs again; this time they flashed their pistols at me outside of this one bar. So I maneuvered away from them again. I had a million thoughts racing in my head. I couldn't run from them, and I began boosting my psyche. No way can I let him get away with my money.

So I went to the store to get a pack of cigarettes, and I saw him pumping gas at the same store. I pointed and aimed, and I shot and killed this young man. To this day I wish I could definitely turn the clock back. I have a few friends who have been gunned down, and it makes me depressed that I have put myself in that pair of shoes. It doesn't make me feel very good about myself at all. So I was convicted of second-degree murder, and I will always remember what I have done and the effect I had on the community.

My life is no textbook story. I come from a middle-class, well-to-do family. Our parents' house is worth $180,000. I have never been poor, but I prefer to be around the poor instead of my own social class. That was the way I was twelve years ago.

Now I pledge to devote my life to doing the right thing before it is too late. Why I thought it was cool to sell drugs and why I was turned off to education, I don't know. No matter what happened in my past, I have learned my lesson. I now know what my goals are, and I control my own destiny. I hate no one. I have learned that life is very precious and valuable. I attempt every waking moment to be productive, whether it be mentally or physically. I am 33 years old now, and all the hoopla on the streets is out of my system. I see some of the kids now who remind me of how I was when I was their age. I tell them with as much passion as I can muster that they are playing Russian roulette with their lives.

CRITICAL THINKING QUESTIONS

1. How would you explain the delinquent behavior of this person?
2. What actually led to the shooting in which he took the life of another?
3. When this person is released from prison, what do you anticipate will happen to him?
4. For him to turn his life around in the community when he is released from prison, what needs to take place?

NOTES

NOTES

NOTES